SACRED SPACES

GUIDE TO CREATING YOUR PERSONAL ALTAR
FOR RITUALS AND REFLECTION

ELEMENTAL MAGIC SERIES
BOOK 14

MONIQUE JOINER SIEDLAK

OSHUN
PUBLICATIONS
oshunpublications.com

Ancient Magick for Today's Witch Series

SACRED SPACES

A Guide to Creating Your Personal Altar for Rituals and Reflection

MONIQUE JOINER SIEDLAK

OSHUN
PUBLICATIONS
oshunpublications.com

Cover Design by MJS

Cover Images by MidJourney

Published by Oshun Publications

www.oshunpublications.com

ANCIENT MAGICK FOR TODAY'S WITCH SERIES

The *Ancient Magick for Today's Witch Series* is a series for modern witches to explore ancient magick, covering Celtic, Gypsy, and Crystal magic, among others. It offers practical advice on spells, rituals, and enchantments for today's use, incorporating natural energies and spiritual connections. With insights into Shamanism, Wicca, and more, it helps readers enhance their magickal journey, offering paths to protection, prosperity, and spiritual growth by combining ancient wisdom with contemporary practice.

Wiccan Basics

Candle Magick

Wiccan Spells

Love Spells

Abundance Spells

Herb Magick

Moon Magick

Creating Your Own Spells

Gypsy Magic

Protection Magick

Celtic Magick

Shamanic Magick

Crystal Magic

Sacred Spaces

Solitary Witchcraft

Novice Witch's Guide

CONTENTS

INTRODUCTION

As soon as I discovered Wicca, I was drawn to the idea of the Sabbats, the colors, and the altar. My home became a sanctuary. One of my first spells was a simple healing spell. I cast a circle around myself. I visualized myself seated at the circle's center as I stood still. As I thought, I saw an image of Mother Earth in her natural state, her hair free-flowing, and some orange and red leaves adorning the tresses. The energy flowed into my eyes and my head, and goosebumps appeared as the hair on my arms stood up. A warm sensation passed from my ears to my hands and toes. I sent some of it back to Mother Earth to give thanks. Wicca reveres humanity and nature; the altar is its most visible manifestation.

Collaboration holds human society together and is the key to our collective success. It can be seen as a map that calls for a sense of self. That we are part of nature does not change, and no matter how much technology changes, we strive to be a part of something, bringing purpose to our lives. I have always been intrigued by the idea of altars and their significance. The various incarnations of an altar I have created for my friends have always been appreciated and enjoyed. Suddenly, I felt as if I had honed and shaped my calling.

Consider your altar to be your center, your oneness. Through it, you are creating multiple facets of yourself. My friends often bombard me with questions about making their altars stand out. I always knew that I had a particular flair/passion for my work, no matter the occasion or the size. Each altar was special to me. My first altar was a simple travel altar. It was so small that it fits inside a red three-ring pencil pouch. I often carried it inside my journal of spells or notebook. I would practice wherever I could, whether in a changing room, the bathroom, or a library study room. The last time I used the travel altar, I was banned from the library for setting off the fire alarm!

Until recently, Wicca was only a tiny private faith, with practitioners keeping the faith's lore a closely guarded secret from the general public. Access to open dialogue and education about Wicca's true meaning has led to a significant change in opinion, personally and within families. It has been my experience that we can find our connection wherever we wish, whether that be a journey to Ireland, Scotland, England, Rome, a coven right around the corner, or online. And it opens up new possibilities for our practices, understandings, and discussions to grow and improve. Assume we choose this option. Today, we can access and learn many things from the world. It is beautiful in more ways than one, but remember that faith is based on authentic principles that are far more important than going viral, and increasing your follower count is essential. There are many ways to connect with the divine forces in the universe and your deeper self. You might be able to eliminate that odd feeling of discomfort when you stand in that one corner of your apartment with a bit of light sage smudging. When you sit before your altar, you might find yourself making different choices or receiving the courage to believe in yourself and what lies ahead.

It might make you laugh and have fun. Maybe you'll cast a love spell over your friend before her blind date, and they'll instantly fall in love. It could be just a tingle, a hint of something supernatural, something unexplainable but undeniable. If so, Wicca and witchcraft can help you become the influential, magical, spiritual person you are.

1

THE ORIGINS AND REASON FOR THE WICCAN ALTAR

Have you ever noticed a small table, shelf, or space in someone's home adorned with candles, flowers, and other objects of reverence? That, my friend, is an altar. Altars have been used centuries as sacred spaces for prayer, meditation, and worship. They come in various shapes, sizes, and styles. Still, their purpose remains the same across cultures and religions: to connect us with the divine.

Picture this: a serene space where you can connect with your inner self, attune with nature's energies, and embark on a transformative spiritual journey. Enter the mystical world of the Wiccan altar. The intricate designs and carefully placed items radiate an aura of wisdom, beckoning you to delve deeper into its history and purpose.

In this article, we will journey together through the origins and reasons behind the Wiccan altar, exploring its rich cultural roots and uncovering its benefits for spiritual practice and self-reflection.

A Timeless Tradition across Cultures and Religions

Ancient Altars

Before the Wiccan altar emerged, altars played a significant role in various cultures and religions. The ancient Mesopotamians, Egyptians, Romans, and Greeks all built sacred altars for rituals, offerings, and communication with the divine. These altars, often adorned with intricate carvings and symbols, were focal points for spiritual practice and served as a bridge between the earthly and celestial realms. And over time, the practice evolved to incorporate personal devotion and reflection.

Religious Altars

The tradition of religious altars has been prevalent throughout history and across various cultures and religions. Altars hold a special place in the hearts of the faithful, as they are seen as a physical manifestation of their devotion to their deity. Altars vary across religions, but the concept remains a sacred place where one can connect with the divine.

What Altars Are Like In Modern Times

Christianity: Altars are central to Christian worship, where the Eucharist, or Communion, is celebrated. In Catholicism, altars are adorned with candles, crucifixes, and statues of saints. Protestants have simpler altars, with a cross or a Bible as the focal point.

Buddhism: In the Buddhist tradition, altars are called Butsudan and are used for offerings, meditation, and prayer. They typically feature a statue or image of the Buddha, incense, and flowers.

Hinduism: Hinduism centers its worship around altars, which can be found in both temples and homes. Unlike temple altars that require a priest for arrangement, home altars are typically created by the house's inhabitants, usually featuring photos or figurines of gods and goddesses.

Judaism: Jewish tradition holds the altar in reverence, perceiving it as a spiritual link between Heaven and Earth. It is seen as the Lord's table and the hub of temple worship, where one can pray, make covenants, and offer sacrifices while connecting to God's presence.

Paganism: In Paganism, altars are used for connecting with nature and the divine. They are often decorated with crystals, herbs, and symbols of the elements.

Islam: Some Islamic cultures and mosques incorporate mihrabs as a focal point of prayer, usually ornately embellished with intricate designs like geometric art or calligraphy.

Religious altars serve as a physical representation of the spiritual connection that we have with our respective deities. It is a tradition that has been practiced for centuries, and its beauty lies in its simplicity and versatility.

THE WICCAN ALTAR: AN INTERSECTION OF NATURE, SPIRITUALITY, AND PERSONAL GROWTH

A Brief History of the Wiccan Altar

The Wiccan altar emerged in the mid-20th century with the rise of contemporary Paganism and Wicca. Drawing inspiration from ancient cultures and pre-Christian traditions, the Wiccan altar fuses elements of nature, spirituality, and personal growth.

Unlike traditional altars, the Wiccan altar is not reserved for worship. Still, it serves as a sacred space for practitioners to connect with the divine, nature, and themselves.

The Elements of a Wiccan Altar

Wiccans have several altar options for their rituals. The materials used for their altars may vary based on the ritual type.

However, a Wiccan altar typically includes the following:

- Tools and symbols representing the four elements (Earth, Air, Fire, and Water)

- The God and Goddess
- The practitioner's intentions

Other items found on a Wiccan altar are candles, incense, a chalice, an athame (ritual knife), a pentacle (a five-pointed star enclosed in a circle), and sometimes personal items.

The Benefits of Having a Personal Altar for Spiritual Practice and Self-Reflection

An altar, a sacred space dedicated to spiritual practice and self-reflection, is significant in various religious and spiritual traditions. Its benefits can extend to individuals from diverse belief systems.

A personal altar can provide a sanctuary for spiritual growth, self-discovery, and emotional well-being. Here are some of the main benefits:

Enhanced Focus and Intentionality

Creating a personal altar allows you to concentrate on your spiritual goals and aspirations and the specific intentions you wish to manifest. Setting up and maintaining your altar requires intentionality and dedication, which fosters a deeper connection to your spiritual practice. By consciously choosing the items and symbols that resonate with you, you invest in your spiritual journey and ensure that your practice remains centered and purposeful.

A Dedicated Space for Meditation and Contemplation

A personal altar serves as a designated space for meditation and contemplation, free from the distractions of daily life. Whether you prefer a small corner of your room or an entire room devoted to your practice, having a separate space for your spiritual endeavors encourages mindfulness and a regular meditation routine. As a result, it is easier to quiet your mind, develop your intuition, and explore your inner world.

Personalized Spiritual Expression

An altar allows you to personalize your spiritual practice by incorporating symbols, elements, and objects of personal significance. This creative process allows you to access your innermost desires, beliefs, and values, cultivating a deeper awareness of yourself and your spiritual path. Your altar expresses your unique spirituality by curating a space that resonates with you. It serves as a steady reminder of your commitment to personal growth.

Emotional Healing and Stress Relief

As a safe space for reflection and introspection, your personal altar can facilitate emotional healing and stress relief. Regular meditation and self-reflection allow you to gain insights into your emotions, thoughts, and patterns, helping you navigate life's challenges with greater clarity and resilience.

The serenity of your altar space can also provide a calming refuge from the stresses of daily life, allowing you to recharge your emotional and spiritual batteries.

Strengthening Your Connection to the Divine

Regardless of your beliefs, a personal altar can help you cultivate a stronger connection to the divine, the universe, or your higher self. Creating a space that honors your spiritual journey opens the door for communication and guidance from the unseen world. This connection can provide valuable insights, wisdom, and support as you navigate your spiritual path.

Should You Have a Personal Altar?

Having a personal altar offers numerous benefits for individuals. Creating a space dedicated to spiritual exploration can strengthen your connection to the divine, deepen your meditation practice, and foster a greater sense of inner peace and balance.

The choice is up to you – whether you choose to set up an altar or not, the important thing is that you remain steadfast in your commitment to your spiritual journey. Whatever form your practice takes, self-discovery is a rewarding and life-changing experience. May your altar serve as a reminder of the beauty and power of the spiritual path.

3

THE ROLE AND PRACTICE OF ALTARS IN WICCAN RITUALS

Setting up your altar is an intuitive process. You should select a place in your home that feels right to you. Ultimately, the more present, spiritually connected, and joyful you feel in a space, the better. Consider a table, a windowsill, a space outside in your garden, or any nook in your house. The ideal location for such a space is somewhere you can sit comfortably and without distraction. The altar can be small, or it can span an entire room. The secret is in using it. You can make your altar as minimal or lavish as you desire—whatever suits you.

Altars are a form of creative expression. It's crucial to tune in to your intuition and intentions and create from this place. As this is the case, stick with what feels right. Your setup may vary. If you prefer, though, you may keep it the same. If this is your choice, stick with what resonates with you. You decide. As long as it's a flat surface, you can use a makeup case, a small shelf, a corner of the floor, an old shoebox, or a cookie tin on top of a dresser. Candles or lights (perhaps inside your Goddess or animal totem) often represent the fire; incense symbolizes the air; sticks or stones represent the earth, as do leaves, herbs, or flowers. Perrier bottles or glass jars are suitable containers for holding water. If you cannot find the elements or are pressed for time, you can use a picture or drawing to illustrate the features. Using the four elements on an altar brings the energies associated with each component to your sacred space. As such, the balance enters your realms and flows through you. As a symbol of self-care, your altar represents you. Dusty, unkempt altars often indicate a need for self-reflection. You can enhance the magic of your altar by showering it with love.

Centeredness creates positive energy and happiness in our lives. Aren't we all striving for that? Our collective unconscious urges us to construct our altar as our ancestors did. Rarely do we pause long enough to listen to the collective unconscious. It is as if collections of wigs, shoes, or records, a wall of beer cans, a shelf of model cars, or a bunch of fancy Pokemon cards are attempts by humans to tap into ancient magical knowledge. Hoping they will aid us, we group our family photos to serve as remembrances of the dead, as a tangible link between the deceased and the living. The practice of creating informal altars crosses cultural and social boundaries. Without realizing it, we are creating altars all around us. We might benefit from giving more thought to this process and learning how to improve our everyday lives and personal growth. Researchers have found very early examples of permanent sacred altars in caves, with narrow, treacherous paths leading to them. Caves were held to be spiritual places that symbolized the eternal and ever-flowing womb of the Goddess and cauldrons of primordial energy.

What do we do in our homes? For spiritual growth and comfort, we create altars. Here, the collective unconscious mind still influences the creation of altars. We draw on the subconscious to build informal altars consisting of collections of items that appeal to it. Thoughtfully designed altars can add positive energy to our lives. When a sacred place is created, it allows us to glimpse wonder. By creating an altar (or altars) in your home, you can fill it with a sense of sacredness, as an altar makes any space sacred. The creation of an altar allows you to receive guidance from the spiritual realm, regardless of which path you follow. It permits you to express your vision of the divine in any way you wish. Creating an altar will help you integrate the sacred into your personal life. It is a place for centering and rebalancing, making you more receptive to your subconscious thoughts.

As a tip, consider placing on it your totems to represent each of the corresponding elements and their related directions. For example, your earth should be north or at the top of the altar. Your air symbol is in the east, at the right. Your fire symbol is in the south, at the bottom. Lastly, your water symbol is in the west, at the left. In the center, you may wish to place something to symbolize the spirit's role in the world to combine with the four other elements. It can be anything you want, such as a crystal or other special object. It needs to be sacred to you.

Building an altar with a deliberate intention can create a positive, spiritual atmosphere that will enhance the quality of your daily life. By deciding to build an altar, you express your wish to connect with the endless source of cosmic energy that supports all life in the universe. You may wish to manifest a particular desire in your life or express your gratitude for what you own. It helps construct your altars with conscious intent and understanding of your actions. Creating an altar on purpose allows you to step away from yourself and whatever problems you may meet daily. Using an altar enables you to elevate your vision to see your surroundings. In addition, it helps you clarify what you are seeking and the reasons you desire it. You may have chosen the objects for your altar but have yet to fully understand why you selected them. Still, creating your altar teaches you to listen to your subconscious mind.

4

THE SACRED TOOLS OF WICCA

Nothing is more magical or meaningful than creating an altar to display all your favorite significant, spiritual, and mystical items for all to see. Your glimpse of the divine can be conveyed on whatever path you choose. Creating an altar gives you access to the spiritual world in whatever way you imagine. Altars serve as places of centering and rebalancing. Incorporating the sacred into your daily life stimulates your subconscious and makes you more open to the holiness of life.

The Following Are Some Examples of Meaningful Items for Your Altar

- Pictures of objects that remind you of what you're manifesting
- Favorite books
- A notepad or journal
- Pictures of your relatives
- Statues
- Crystals

- A meditation cushion or rug
- Tarot and oracle cards
- Incense
- Candles
- Slips of paper with rituals, spells, or prayers written on them
- Flowers

A symbol of protection should always be on your altar, such as a white and/or a red candle (one of each is preferred). The colors white and red protect against negativity. Light your altar's candle(s) daily during meditation to ramp up its protective powers. In addition to black salt and pyrite, a piece of tourmaline quartz and a decorative jar is also recommended. Does create an altar and establishing a sacred space require certain specific materials? Not necessarily. You can use whatever you have on hand. Look around. Who knows what you'll find? How will you arrange your symbols?

Dishes

Maybe you're content with a saucer or a simple trinket dish. If not, it's easy to find dishes as unique as you are. I will help spark your imagination with a few descriptions of charismatic options.

What exact dish should you buy?

Do you envision a handmade piece about 2 cm thick and 14 cm long, a quirky original work—a crescent moon–shaped earthenware piece with a hand-painted image of a moon goddess inside?

The pentagram is a powerful symbol of faith, a symbol of the five elements—spirit, earth, air, fire, and water. It accommodates five tea-light candles made of resin and a circle representing the universe. Maybe something painted black.

Here's a rare find—a silky-smooth vessel with ridged edges, a place to hold your rolled intentions or crystals. A stone leaf jar can be a shrine jar or a stone altar dish adorned with gold leaves, stones, and pebbles.

Rare is debonair, but what's an altar dish if it's not vintage? Consider a vintage brass altar plate that doubles as an offering dish or smudge plate. Even if your altar is tiny, this gorgeous addition will fit—12.5 cm or 5 inches in diameter.

To be ruled and one with the moon at any time of the year is a charm. How about a small altar plate with blue-purple transitions in varying light and a floral pentagram design? Always feel the beautiful aura of the moon when you hold this plate.

Cloths

Most Wiccans use an altar cloth when arranging their altars. Generally, an altar cloth serves two purposes: to protect anything placed on the altar from damage and to increase the power or intent of the magic. Consider whether a particular altar cloth could bolster ideas or abilities you wish to invoke. Anything goes! Fabrics such as cotton, silk, bamboo fiber, and wool are all great options. I buy organic cotton or wild silk to stay ethical and sustainable. Pick a material that feels great in your hands, and that you enjoy holding. Don't add it to your altar if you don't like how it feels! Mint green is my favorite color, and I adore using it when creating magic. The cheesy grin and the fluttery feeling that came over me when I first discovered my handmade mint-green satin charmeuse tarot cloth empowered me. My cyclical nature was reflected in the snake eating its tail and in the moon phases. I felt a connection

with the feminine energy within me. It was absolutely gorgeous
—so many beautiful details. I bought two for my tarot spreads.
When choosing an altar cloth, the color you select has great
meaning. Some colors correspond to the eight different Sabbats
on the Wheel of the Year, and there are also general meanings
for colors in Wicca.

- Imbolc—white, Uranian blue, orchid pink, or pink
  lavender
- Ostara—pale yellow, white, peachy pink, tan, or beige
- Beltane—light greens, blues, yellows, pinks, or white
- Litha—strong yellows, greens, reds, or golds
- Lammas—raw sienna, burnt umber, Indian red or
  yellow ochres
- Mabon—rust, marigold, deep navy, burnt-sienna
  brown, terra-cotta, sage, or turmeric
- Samhain—grays, blacks, dark blues, or orange
- Yule—red, silver, gold, white, or green

Suppose you're overwhelmed by using a different cloth every
Sabbat. In that case, you can decorate your altar cloth with
colors representing the four seasons. If you want to make your
Wiccan altar cloth yourself, do it—it's effortless! You can
choose a beautiful fabric you love or an old shirt with sentimental value cut into the size you need. I prefer to hem mine so
that it looks neat. Occasionally, I embroider items and add
charms to my altar cloths using hemp, thread, or plastic lace.
As a bonus, you can also paint, print, or stitch onto your altar
cloth or choose a plain one. Why limit yourself to just one?
Nothing stops you from making as many as your heart desires
to switch around whenever you want.

Candles

Abra-candle-abra. Abra-candle-abra. Abra-candle-abra. Abra-candle-abra. The more candles I can place on my altar, the happier I am. Candle colors can also help to enhance your altar. You can select candles that are appropriate for specific purposes or events. For the winter solstice, you may use gold, silver, or yellow candles, while green and pink candles aid in finding love (and increasing your wealth). Candles symbolize fire and the south. As part of the Wiccan tradition, many candles are lit and placed on an altar representing gods and goddesses.

Do you want to catch your wax? Or would you rather clean up any wax pools? Consider placing your candle in a holder or snuffer to prevent dripping pools on your altar. You can use chime candleholders or tea-light candles for more minor spells. When performing large spells that require many candles, having multiple candleholders may not be cost-effective. On a plate or tray, heat the bottom of the candle until the wax begins to melt, place it on the plate until it has cooled, and secure it safely. If it fails, try again. Sand or salt in a bowl can also be used as a candle base. To keep your candle upright, you will need enough to cover your candle's bottom inch or two.

Incense and Smudge Sticks

Traditionally, smudges are made from a bundle of magical herbs whose smoke, when burned, is used to cleanse, sanctify, and bless a person, a place, or a thing. Sage, cedar, lavender, and sweetgrass are other herbs. You can buy sticks that are already made that have various plants in them. Or you can make your own. Read on!

Cultivating Plants: Binding the Herbs

When you harvest plants for smudging or any other ritual, you should ask the plant for its cooperation and leave an offering. Failure to do so can channel negative energy. An offering is essential for ritual objects because it is a way to show respect to the plant and soothe its spirit. Choose which herbs will suit your needs based on their qualities.

Smudging is its own ritual. It can be messy, so you should put something like a piece of parchment paper or a sheet underneath you to make cleanup easier. After gathering the herbs, bind them in a sacred space. Scissors and thread are also needed.

A natural embroidery thread or quilting thread would be ideal. A thin thread, such as that used for sewing, can cut into the herbs and break them rather than bind them. Choose something made of linen, cotton, or hemp that is not dyed. Remember, you will be burning this and inhaling it! The last thing you want is to pollute the energy—or your sacred body—with chemicals.

If you can, choose threads dyed with natural plant colors. You might wrap your herbs in a green cord if you want health. As you tie the herbs, please pay attention to what energies they contain. Imagine that the thread is binding the magic into your bundle. Say a blessing or prayer over your herbs when you're finished, dedicating it to its purpose. Be grateful for the gift the plant and the Mother have given you.

Smudge Burning

Burn herbs in the following manner. First, crumble or shave bits of the herb onto an ignited charcoal block. Alternatively, you can light the smudge stick (or sweetgrass braid). I prefer to light them from my altar candle; I feel that the divine energy is symbolic and practical—symbolic because I am nurturing and transferring the flame (spirit) from one entity to another and practical as it can take a while for the herbs to catch. A candle flame is a continuous safe source of the fire.

Since sweetgrass braids tend to be hard to light, light the thin end and gently fan the sweetgrass braid up and down to help it burn. Light a smudge stick at the top, as it's the thinner and less twisted end. Make sure you don't blow on the smoke. With a feather, fan the smoke over yourself or the object you are smudging. In your mind, let go of anything not serving your best interests and visualize a cloud of smoke. See the smoke rising upward and taking your ills with it. The energies are retransformed into positive energy by the sacred smoke. They return to the source. Meditate, pray, sing, play music, or have your favorite show or movie playing in the background. If you prefer silence, allow the sounds of birds chirping or kids playing outside, and let the feeling of cleansing take root. You can keep a bowl of sand or earth nearby. It would be best if you buried the burning end entirely after you have finished smudging. Check back to make sure it is completely out. This bowl is also helpful for tapping loose burning embers into.

Incense

Scent can be influential in spiritual pursuits. Most religions use incense as a heavenly aroma. Incense comes in various forms, such as cones, sticks, or powder. Many types of incense are made with chemical fragrances and fillers rather than organic ingredients, which can pose problems or dangers to witches. Look for all-natural incense.

Blessed Be, Safety First

Using a fire-safe cauldron with sand at the bottom is a good idea if you are burning things. The fabric underneath or hanging sleeves may catch fire due to heat. Be careful of nearby flammables as well. Remember that too much smoke will set off a smoke detector if you smudge or use incense indoors. In dry weather, be very careful when smudging outdoors. Forest or grass fires are not a respectful way to honor the Mother.

Ritual of Smudging

To perform a smudging ritual, you will need the following:

- Lighter Or Matches
- Candles
- Shell or Fireproof Receptacle
- Sage Bundle

Let's begin!

Set your intention, say a prayer, and then light your candle upon your altar; as you meditate, ask the universe to surround and guide your space with love and openness.

Let the red glow of the embers enchant you; as a caution, when the ashes start falling, hold your fireproof container beneath them to catch the ash. Light your sage from your candle, matches, or a lighter.

Out loud, say a variation of a cleansing incantation. It could be something like "Sage, assist me as I cleanse this space and my tools of any adverse spirits," or "Sanctify, dispel, forgive. Fire to air, air to water, water to earth." Whatever spell you choose, visualize your space's idea, clear any negative energy, and open it to the positive.

Fan the smoke from the sage over your altar and tools, continuing to visualize the smoke, cleansing the space of any antagonistic vibrancy.

Having purified your altar, the last thing you'll need to do to finish setting it up is to meditate and set your intention, visualizing the excellent work you'll do there. Recite a short prayer: "Invoking the powers of fire, I summon the protector and the guardian to escort me from all that would harm me, whether bodily, psychologically, mentally, or otherwise."

Can't wait to practice with your altar, right? May you be blessed!

Herbs and Plants

It's your altar, but here are some characteristics traditionally attributed to various flowers and herbs to help you channel and personify different energies throughout the year. Once you learn to make incense, you can often modify the list to fit your style. Incense recipes may require you to keep some herbs nearby to create custom blends.

Plants

Acorns—longevity and stamina

Basil—independence and freedom from inertia

Cinnamon—purification, and healing

Elderberries—safeguard against evil and negativity

Ferns—earnestness and industriousness

Heather—wish fulfillment and preservation

Jasmine—compassion, romance, and genuine love

Lavender—elimination of apathy

Oak—soundness, sturdiness, and resilience

Poppies—bliss and contentment

Rose—generosity and grace

Sage—everlasting health and happiness

Thyme—awakening and renewal

What you choose is entirely up to you. Each element can have one item: earth may be represented by a clump of soil or a piece of a beehive, fire by a flame or a string of Christmas lights; you can have a photo of water, or you can pour some into a travel-size bottle with alcohol (from a favorite vacation) or blessed water; and air can be smudge or incense.

Herbs

Allspice—finances and wealth

Arabic Gum—sound reasoning, refinement, and fortification

Basil—preservation and security (traditionally used for making holy water in Greek Orthodox churches)

Bay Leaves—repelling evil interference

Benzoin—cosmic illuminations and purification

Camphor—prophecy, spiritual abilities, and sanctification

Cedar—capital, providing shelter and abundance, refining and healing

Cinnamon—intercosmic calculations, devotion, ardor, assets, preservation, prognostication, and purification

Cloves—warding off evil and illicit desires and strengthening relationships

Copal—exorcism, love, protection, and purification

Dragon's Blood—abolishment of glamour's and bolstering of affluence

Frankincense—catharsis, deliverance, expulsion, shielding, and indemnity

Juniper Berries—the cultivation of psychic proficiency, fostering of passion, and imparting of protection

Lavender—devotion and adoration, goodwill, refuge, guidance, salvation, and absolution

Mugwort—strengthening of the power of ritual tools (collect the leaves during the full summer moon)

Myrrh—atonement, purification, and spiritual strength

Orange Peel—love, improvement of finances, divination, and telepathy

Patchouli—removal of curses, winning back lost love, the defeat of enemies, and healing of grief

Pine—cleanliness and refreshment, purification of one's atmosphere

Rosemary Leaves—remembrance, fidelity, the faithfulness of a lover

Rose Petals—love, protection

Rue—repentance, freedom, and protection against evil spirits

Sage—wisdom and long life

Sandalwood (yellow)—protection, illumination, and an exorcism tool

Thyme—combating negativity and depression; also an aphrodisiac

Tobacco—purification

Vervain—love, money, protection, rebirth, and redemption

Wormwood—safety and clairvoyance

Crystals and Stones

Healing is all about balancing the body. The vibrational frequency of crystals enhances healing. Crystals can be beneficial in balancing your energy and revitalizing you when you are stressed. Align your frequency with crystals that can create healing and balance. It will take time. Treatments are different in length and frequency. Wicca utilizes the world's natural resources for numerous purposes, including health, magical rituals, meditation, and manifestation. People have been drawn to rocks, stones, and crystals for eons, believing they have magical properties; the ancient Egyptians used turquoise, lapis lazuli, and clear quartz for healing and protection. Crystals each have their own energies and vibrational properties. You can benefit from crystals throughout your home and carry crystals with you to improve your mood and aid in physical, mental, and spiritual healing.

Using Crystals in Wicca

Crystals possess both magical and healing properties. It is common for people to carry crystals with them, wear them as talismans to protect themselves from evil spirits or make jewelry containing energy. Certain crystals can strengthen your focus. While meditating, you may choose a crystal related to the issue you are trying to resolve. Your thoughts will become more transparent, and you will be able to guide yourself properly. Spells and rituals that utilize crystals can be highly effective. They can be used to create or change something and even to infuse potions with power. Crystals can also serve as protective objects around the house. Divination utilizes crystals to focus energies and to make divination tools, such as rune stones, pendulums, scrying mirrors, and crystal balls.

Crystal Awareness: Knowing the Right One

The crystal I select could be one I have already looked at, one that comes to mind, or one that hadn't previously attracted me but now does. Every crystal has distinctive characteristics, and each one catches my attention in a new way. I may examine a crystal with properties relevant to what I am currently struggling with. When I buy crystals, I tend to imagine how they will feel and bond; if possible, I cradle them for a few moments before buying them to ensure they feel right to me. Let's begin by looking at the most common crystals used for spell work, meditation, and divination.

Specific Crystals and Stones

Abalone Shell—reduction of stress and calming of the mind

Agate—concentration, healing, soothing

Atlantean Seed—harmony (when spun in the sunlight, these prismatic crystals emit a rainbow of colors and a harmonic resonance)

Amazonite—unity and integration

Amber—security, comfort, and soothing

Amethyst—relaxation, healing, and sleep

Angel Aura Quartz—harmony, peace, and spirituality

Apatite—inspiration, spiritual awakening, psychic ability, communication, extroversion

Apophyllite—innate wisdom and intuition

Aquamarine—self-expression, meditation, and calming

Aventurine—mental and emotional clarity, a positive attitude, alignment, independent thinking, alleviation of anxiety and fear

Black Tourmaline—balance and promotion of positive energy

Bloodstone—vitality and well-being

Blue Agate—healing, communication, and stability

Blue Quartz—promotion of order and soothing

Carnelian—creativity, attentiveness, prosperity, nourishment of sensitive dispositions, inspirations of openness and curiosity

Celestite—anxiety relief

Chalcopyrite—dispersion of stagnant energy, inspiration, and widening of intuition, the attraction of (informational) ethereal energies to you and through you to others

Chrysoprase—positive vibrations and overall wellness

Citrine—clarity of thought, self-esteem, harmony, imagination, intellect, self-confidence, connection to one's highest self

Danburite—tranquil sleep, vivid dreams, spiritual and emotional recovery, optimism, dispersion of past pain, enhancement of awareness

Devic Temple Crystals—attraction of higher dimensional gateways; facilitation of lifting the veil between the worlds and allowing spiritual energies to roam the physical plane

Diamond—drive, determination, self-confidence, creativity, and perseverance

Dumortierite—healing potential, mental clarity, optimism, and strength

Elestials—the transformation of negative beliefs, clearing of obstructions and toxicity, imparting of guidance, and alignment with the subconscious

Emerald—psychic ability, prosperity, compassion, patience, physical and emotional healing, serenity, calmness, clarity, and love

Fluorite—reduction of the air's psychic clutter, enhancement of perception and concentration, meditation, and higher self-awareness

Fuchsite—invigoration, revitalization, and enhancement of communication

Galena—a grounding stone, a spiritual guide; enhancement of emotional growth, upliftment, and safeguard from electromagnetic interference

Garnet—vitality, insight, empathy, mindfulness, prosperity, the balance of self-esteem and willpower

Goldstone—intuition, inner strength, and total wellness

Hematite—stress relief, restoration of equilibrium, and enhancement of concentration

Herkimer Diamond—a storage medium; clairvoyance and dreamwork, stress relief, and dispersion of negative energies

Jade—longevity, money, and business; strengthening of connections with nature; a shield against negative influences

Jasper—a rubbing stone is worn for the removal of negative energy and entity attachments, promotion of reassurance and serenity

Kyanite—an energy conduit capable of balancing most body systems; creative expression, communication, and astrological projection

Labradorite—an aid in seeing past illusions to uncover your true dreams; boost intuition and creativity. Stimulate creativity, enthusiasm, and goal achievements. Promotion of meditation and new ideas

Lapis Lazuli—intuition, easing of tension and anxiety, creation of balance and clarity

Law Twin—alignment of the aura with one's more profound matter, dispersion of anger, and restoration of hope

Malachite—balance and harmony, stress relief, elimination of nightmares, augmentation and expansion of awareness and expression

Moonstone—good fortune (especially in business), inner strength and courage, discernment, intuition, restoration of relationships, and absorption of illnesses and pain

Obsidian—easing of tensions, dissolution of repressed mental blocks, the release of emotions with understanding and love; excellent for grounding spiritual energy into the physical realm

Peridot—positivity, patience, abundance, clarity, and clairvoyance

Pyrite—unmasking of good hidden energy, absorption of negative energy, assistance in overcoming inertia and feelings of inadequacy

Rhodochrosite —promotion of natural androgyny and self-identification, strengthening of memory and intellect

Ruby—self-confidence, courage, spiritual balance, adaptability, enthusiasm, commitment, and leadership qualities

Sapphire—fuel for the ability to express oneself, promotion of wellness and good feelings, communication with the spirits

Serpentine—an excellent tool for healing loss, separation, and betrayal

Spirit Quartz—detoxification, spiritual growth, and connection

Staurolite—protection, enlightenment, stabilization of emotions, aid in finding lost items

Tiger's Eye—emotional balance, courage, self-confidence, willpower

Unakite—an aid in casting magic spells with confidence; the revelation of deception

Vesuvianite—an aid in finding a valid path in life; alignment of the will with the heart, provision of courage for change, and release of negative attachments

Zircon—intensification of emotional equilibrium and confidence, similar to diamonds and quartz crystals

Crystal Cleaning

Crystals store energy. A magical bond is created as they collect the earth's power and others' energies. You can cleanse them as frequently as you feel necessary. It's probably best to cleanse them before incorporating them into your magical workings. You can use the following methods to cleanse your crystals:

- Burn sage or incense, and let the smoke of the sage envelop the crystal. Swish it around in the smoke.
- Research the crystals you will cleanse with water before using them. Some suitable water sources include waterfalls, lakes, rivers, streams, oceans, and streams.
- Bury the crystals in the ground for at least 12 hours. In the evening, store your crystals in a safe location outside for the night, and allow their natural energy to charge them.
- Meditate with the crystals, and clear them with your intuition. When cleansing your crystals, blow gently.

Oils, Potions, and Brews

Anoint candles with oils before lighting them. Rub the oil on the candle from wick to end when you want to attract something. Or, to repel, rub the opposite way. Add a few drops of essential oil to your chime or votive candle to enhance your spells. Pick a bigger candle, such as a seven-day candle, for spells lasting a few days.

Amber (earthy, sweet, and smooth)—success and good fortune

Bayberry (earthy and spicy)—traditional in money-drawing spells and rituals and a favorite scent of the Yule season

Bergamot (bright and fresh)—money and success

Carnation (floral and sweet)—a healing and strength essential

Cinnamon (spicy and earthy)—attraction and speed

Heliotrope (earthy and floral)—healing and wealth

Juniper (earthy and spicy)—love and protection

Lotus (floral, bright, and earthy)—protection, healing, and spirituality

Musk (smooth, sweet, and masculine)—attraction and lust

Ylang-ylang (floral and earthy)—opportunity and peace

A splendid potion or brew demands perfect timing. Magic invokes powerful emotions in our subconscious, regardless of the time of day. The conscious mind is heightened during daylight hours, when our leadership abilities, strength, and vitality are in force. Noon is associated with fire energies, which purify, illuminate, and deal with issues of focus or reason. In the evening, the creative, intuitive, instinctive maternal self is accentuated; sunset symbolizes relaxation and introspection. At midnight, the veil between worlds thins, and magic is unleashed! Dawn represents the beginning of a new chapter, hope for the future, and letting go of the past.

Let me be your voice of reason—don't bother with anything plastic. I wish I'd known not to use plastic when starting out. Losing batches of perfectly blended oils and cleaning oil off my dressers and shelves was an unnecessary headache. Awful. Magic elixirs and oils don't work well in plastic containers. Buy at least seven glass eye droppers; if you can, buy a Pyrex measuring cup for larger batches. (Alternatively, you can repurpose old shot glasses or buy a few mason jars.) Use your intuition and creativity until you achieve the right oil smell when using a Pyrex container to make your oils. Keep a record of everything you do. Knowing the moon phase, the day of the week, the time of day, and the ingredients you use are crucial. That way, you can duplicate the mixture later and not end up with something completely different—a great way to start your journey into harnessing your magical power and energy. I hope this will help you enjoy making magical oils, brews, and potions. Instead of making up your own, you can 'borrow' and hopefully fall in love with a few of my tried-and-true favorites.

Oils

Remember, this oil is for you, and you only, so make it. Enjoy sampling blends. There's no rush. Be aware of allergens, and ensure that oils are safe on the skin. I recommend using a carrier oil, which is a must if you only use essential oils. Choosing a blend containing both a fragrance and essential oils will make your fragrance last longer and help you get maximum enjoyment. Also, consider anointing your favorite crystals, amulets, talismans, and other charms.

Gossamer Wings Oil

- 2 drops of Cajuput
- 3–5 drops of Violet
- 3–5 drops of Lemon
- 3–5 drops of Lavender

You can contact faeries, sylphs, and elves using this oil, who tend to romp through the air element.

All-Night-Long Oil

- 4 drops of Jasmine
- 3 drops of Cinnamon
- 3–5 drops of Vanilla
- 5 drops of Honeysuckle

Oh, jambah-la. So, you've decided you want to party. All night... all night long. This is the perfect oil for those nighttime escapades. Test this oil 48 hours before, as an allergic reaction to the cinnamon is possible. Or add several drops into your bath or massage oil after a rough day.

Happy-Heart Oil

- 2 1/2 ounces of Sweet Almond Carrier Oil
- 3 1/2 tablespoons of Wisteria Flowers

After covering the flowers with oil, let them sit in a dark place for 2 weeks.

Shake them daily. Drain and then bottle.

This oil attracts happiness and good vibrations.

Tea

Brewing magical tea is simple. Just follow these instructions:

1.Bring water to a boil over a stovetop or kettle. Never microwave water.

2.Once the water has reached the boiling point, wait about 45 seconds before pouring it onto the herbs, enhancing steeping. While pouring the water, visualize what you wish to achieve.

3.Allow the tea to steep for 7–11 minutes, depending on your preferred strength.

Tea has potent magic if you enjoy it naturally. But if you hate the taste, the energy of that resistance becomes a more significant issue. Add honey, ginger, orange juice, or sugar mixed with maple syrup.

Magical Evening Tea

Transitioning from the workday to the evening can take a lot of work. I recommend drinking this tea when ready to unwind from a long day and want to get into a relaxed and calm mind-set. Feeling at peace at the end of the day is good!

To prepare this tea, use the following elements:

- 1 teaspoon of Hibiscus
- 1 teaspoon of Lavender
- 3 teaspoons of Chamomile

Combine the herbs in a small bowl, and stir them gently with your fingers before placing them in the mug. Observe how your energy begins to settle as you pour the water over the herbs. Sip the tea and read a chant—your calm energy will soothe you for several hours.

Lucky Prosperity Tea

This fun blend is generally better for daytime use, as it's caffeinated. However, you could also use decaf black (chai) tea. If you usually add milk and sugar to black (chai) tea, do so before adding the herbs. It's meant to be a pleasing, energetic lift.

Gather the following:

- 1 Black (Or Chai) Tea Bag
- 1/2 pinch Of Cinnamon
- 2 pinches of Nutmeg
- 1 pinch of Ginger Powder

Brew the tea, steep for 2 1/2 minutes, then add the ginger powder, cinnamon, and nutmeg. Find a short whimsical luck chant, and read it three times. Be open to receiving the clue that a beautiful surprise is awaiting you. Hold on to this feeling until you are finished drinking. Then, lock this feeling away and forget it, to allow it time to manifest.

An Enchanting a Bath

Incorporating herbs into a ritual bath is a great way to utilize earth energies' magical powers, making your bath a mystical experience. But if you're pressed for time or space, you can use a bucket of hot water and a mug and perform this ritual while you shower! Steep the herbs into the bucket. Then, use the cup to dip into the bucket and pour the water over your body. Infusions are the most popular method; you can incorporate herbs into the water in various ways.

In a large pot, pour boiling water over the herbs. Cover and steep for 25–35 minutes, then strain the water into another container. Another option is to place the herbs in a cloth bag or wrap them in a washcloth (you can tie the washcloth closed with a ribbon). Even a sock will do for this purpose! Place the bundled herbs directly into the tub (or bucket). Finally, it can be a delightful experience to just let the herbs float loosely around you in the water. Only use this method if you have a hair catcher in your drain to prevent the herbs from clogging the pipes when you drain the tub.

Good Vibrations Bath

You will need the following for this positivity-promoting bath:

- 1/2 cup Chamomile Flowers
- 1/4 cup Hibiscus
- 1/4 cup Sea Salt (Or A Few Splashes of Florida Water)
- 1/2 cup Lavender Flowers

This bath is so delightful that you will find yourself instantly able to visualize happiness, tranquility, and a loving feeling in your life. I usually play my favorite 1990s tunes when I draw this bath.

Ahhh. Ahhh. It's about that time to dip your toe in. Feel it... feel it. Feel it—feel that good vibration. Feel that sensation flow into your bones. You can use this combination of herbs to prepare for any magic; it goes particularly well with love spells. The lavender and hibiscus are well suited for inviting loving vibrations into your life. At the same time, the chamomile can help soothe any unsettling emotions. Including sea salt or Florida water will add an extra spark to the overall energy. I suggest placing the hibiscus in an infusion or a cloth bag. Please test a small area first, and avoid putting loose flowers into the water because they tend to stain tubs.

5

TOOLS OF MAGIC FOR THE WICCAN ALTAR

For Wiccans, the altar is a sacred space where they perform rituals and connect with the divine. The tools of magic used on the altar are essential for these practices, as they help channel the practitioner's energy and intention.

Each tool on the altar has a specific purpose and represents a particular element or aspect of the practitioner's spiritual practice.

Using magic tools on the altar helps create a focused and intentional environment for spiritual work. They are physical reminders of the practitioner's connection to the divine and commitment to their spiritual path. Magic tools also add a level of symbolism and ritual to Wiccan practice, helping practitioners connect with the spiritual forces they seek to invoke.

The tools of magic are an integral part of Wiccan practice, and their use on the altar helps create a sacred and intentional space for spiritual work.

Outlined below are some of the more popular tools used by Wiccans.

Athame

Athames are two-edged ritual knives, usually with a dark (or black) handle made of stone, wood, crystal, or metal. They typically measure over 6 in. in length. Symbolically, the two sides represent the God and Goddess, who comes together at the blade's point, at the union of the spiritual and mundane worlds, and in the idea that power, comes with responsibilities. An athame is usually a ritual tool used to cut things metaphorically; it is not typically used to cut things physically. You can buy an athame from pagan shops, magic stores, craft stores, local dollar stores, and antique shops. Some Wiccan traditions hold that if the athame ever draws blood, it must be destroyed, but this is not a universal belief. If you are prone to dropping things, you might want an athame that isn't too sharp. Athames aren't sharp simply because their purpose is to focus and direct energy, especially when drawing circles or calling quarters.

Boline (Utility Knife)

You could keep a utility knife or boline at your altar as a second option. This knife is used to cut raw materials during magical workings. Since an athame cannot be used to cut anything solid, a ritual utility knife is necessary for cutting herbs, plants, flowers, cords, offerings, or anything else you need during ritual or magic or for carving symbols into candles and wands. Only ceremonial and magical rituals should be performed with the utility knife. Some Wiccans prefer crescent-moon blades, small scythes, or scissors. The boline has a lighter handle, usually cream or white in color. Your boline must be sharper than your athame because this knife is for physical cutting. You can make your boline from a regular knife, and then incorporate it into your workings.

Wand

You can make a wand from a thick wooden dowel. You can also use oak, ash, willow, crystal, or stone. Add embellishments like crystals, feathers, string, copper, antlers, bone, silver, or steel, or carve or write relevant symbols on your wand. What matters is how the wand resonates with its owner. A rod is for channeling and projecting our inner light. Instead of cutting wood from a living tree, use a fallen branch. If you wish to thank the tree, give it a compost or water offering. Wands are at least 5 in. long and made from smoothed-down natural materials. They are thicker at the top and taper toward the bottom.

Chalice

A chalice represents the Goddess and the womb. It is a glass, goblet, cup, or sometimes a mug made from silver, gold, metal, clay, or any material safe for drinking that won't leak. Fill the chalice with a liquid offering such as water or wine during rituals. The chalice is associated with water and the west. Your chalice can also be used to keep an offering on Sabbats to honor your deities. A familiar ritual in Wiccan circles involves lowering the athame's blade into the chalice to symbolize the sexual union of the God and Goddess. You can buy specific chalices from pagan shops, or the goblet, such as a stoneware cup, can be much more straightforward. Often you can find great chalices at art fairs and thrift stores.

Cauldrons

Any waterproof pot will work as a cauldron. A big cast-iron pot that stands 3 feet tall is only necessary if it's something you can work with. Mine is only 4 inches. Cauldrons are commonly used to burn stones, oils, or materials for more minor spells or personal use. It symbolizes feminine energy, like the chalice. A pot, firepit, or heated oven may be required for larger projects. Using a tea-light candle to heat your small cauldron is effective. Keep your pot clean and undamaged, just as you would any other magic tool, so no excess energy or physical leftovers from previous workings will affect your future workings. Cauldrons can be found online, in occult shops, or in flea markets. I also like to plan weekends away and shop at rural flea markets. I find the best pieces there.

Broom, Broomstick, Besom

Like those found in craft stores, a Wiccan ritual broom can be ordinary, handmade, or decorative. The broom symbolizes the sexual union of the God and Goddess. It is used to sweep energy out of the circle space before drawing the circle. Wiccans also use the broom to raise energy. We do not use our broom to clean our altar—a common misconception. Instead, we use it to remove (sweep away) unwanted energies around our altar. We can do this before any magical workings or divination.

Additionally, it can be used during rituals to help clear anything that needs clearing. You can bind your broom using twigs that you have collected and dried out. Before being dry and sanded, the twigs must be wrapped securely with string or rope and then dried, sanded, and glossed in much the same way as your wand. The broom is associated either with the earth or with the air.

Bell

Traditionally, keeping a bell at your altar was always very important. Its gentle peals can call upon the deities. The sound can also be used to eliminate any unwanted energy, as the vibrational properties of the bell dispel negative energies. Let your imagination run wild. Any bell works (even a musical doorbell); you can buy a special bell with relevant symbols or just a regular one. Bells made from metal are preferable.

Censer, Herbs, Sage, and Incense

Having herbs at your altar is also a good idea. You can hang them on your wall, a shelf, or a drawer. Each herb can be relevant to the particular creator. You can use it for cleansing and offering to your deities. For example, offer a flower or a flowering plant to a goddess of fertility or love. You may use lavender or roses.

Sage is a fantastic thing to have at your altar—it represents air in magic. If you want to cast a circle, cleanse, or do whatever you need, some dried sage will always be handy.

Incense can be used to represent air. Cleansing and consecrating tools are among its uses. Also, because several scents can relate to specific deities, incense can be used to honor the Sabbats and gods. All herbs and aromas have magical correspondences. Wiccans frequently burn incense in their ritual circles to set the mood and attract the energy they need for their rituals. Wiccans also use incense to purify the ritual space and consecrate items for ritual use by passing them through the smoke. You can use loose incense that you burn on charcoal or sticks or cones inside the censer during your ritual. The censer and incense represent fire and air, south and east.

Statues

Often, witches use statues to represent the God and Goddess on their altars. While not necessary, it adds a sense of sacredness. You can find an assortment of figures online or in occult stores. Use statues instead of candles to call upon specific gods and goddesses. Statues can be made of concrete or stone, bought online or from stores near you, or made from cardboard cutouts, miniature dolls, stickers, or pictures.

Salt and Water

Use natural, unfiltered water for consecrating objects in rituals because it contains vitality. Salt and water are associated with earth and water, north and west. Mix salt water and use it to bless and purify the ritual circle.

Book of Shadows

As the area around your altar usually remains undisturbed, consider keeping your Book of Shadows there. Use it as a journal, writing in it daily or whenever you like. In this book, record your hopes and dreams, the time the twinkle of the moon refracts off your pendant. Record your rituals and spells, whether they were successful, and if they require any improvements. The Book of Shadows can be whatever you like, from a three-ring notebook to a bound blank book. Choose a notebook with aged paper. You can age a book's leaves yourself with tea. Doodle on the cover, or buy one with artwork. Get one with an old binding so it looks like a medieval spellbook. Writing down rituals and techniques that work for you as you explore your path can be helpful.

Pentagram, Inverted Pentagram

As it is the central symbol of Wicca, placing a pentagram at your altar is a good idea. A pentagram symbolizes the five elements. Having one on your altar will also strengthen your incantations and desires. Invoking deities with an athame and wand is often done by tracing or drawing the pentagram. It is also used to cast circles. Pentagrams can be engraved with sticks, wood, or other natural materials. Wicca reveres the pentagram as a symbol of the divine, with the inverted pentagram representing male energies and the upright one representing female energies.

Tools to Implement Prophecy, Bless the Tools and Offerings

In your most sacred space, display your favorite divination tools, such as tarot cards, tasseography teacups, scrying tools, pendulums, or rune stones, and set up an altar. In addition to keeping them connected, this helps the tools become accustomed to your patterns, which helps when it comes to divination, especially when the pieces are new. Connecting with your tools is essential. Whether they're major or minor tools, you want them to be familiar with your patterns. You can do this before cleansing and consecrating them, or you can do it afterward.

Meditate with the tools, or carry them with you in a bag for between 12 and 27 days, sleeping with it near you at night. Once you purchase or make the tools you wish to use for magical purposes, cleansing and consecrating them is paramount. You want to ensure that the tools you use are free of any positive or negative energy they might have picked up from wherever they came from. Clear them, prepare them for use in your practices, and get them used to your patterns and purpose. If the tool has been mishandled, it may need to be cleansed and consecrated again.

Adorn your altar with a variety of offerings. While cleansing, say, "Purify my intentions and tools for all to be clear and blessed within my work." Show your gratitude with herbs, flowers, incense, relevant foods, wines, and water whenever you call on your gods to help with a ritual, spell, or other mystical enterprise. You can find or make the tools that resonate with you more if you acquire them slowly rather than rush out to get them all at once.

6

ALIGNING ENERGIES

Incarnation, abundance, and aligning energies—a manifestation is an act of gaining or changing something in our lives. The act of manifesting abundance is no different, except that we must look at what we already have before we receive more. We must acknowledge, appreciate, and be thankful for what we already have to receive plenty. If you come from self-ishness, your abundance rituals will never work. Abundance is like giving thanks. Let the universe add to your blessings. After calming your mind and calling in your energy and spirit, it is time to focus that energy. The more vivid your manifestation, the more powerful it will be. Meditation allows you to embrace your core and merge your conscious and subconscious minds. It will enable you to change your reality with little more than the power of your thoughts.

Allow yourself 11 minutes to concentrate and center your mind. With this method, you will ensure that you have the time and attention you need to create what you are trying to manifest. You will also give your mind and spirit some time to recover from anything other than the intentions you are about to set. After visualizing it, write this abundance on paper, beginning with a positive 'I' statement such as "I am...." "I can...." "I will...."

I am this abundance.
I have many friends who support me.
I will achieve financial stability and be satisfied with my life.

Fold the paper three times, and burn it in the fire. Close your eyes, and visualize the manifestation you desire. Or, imagine a candle, and list your blessings. Allow the images to reach the flame and then evaporate.

Initiation, or the Beginning of Self-Dedication

When one seeks a new religion or group, they must find a coven that accepts them. The most important part of being a witch is initiating yourself and practicing immediately. This ritual needs to be performed in private, without onlookers. To truly embrace the concept of rebirth, you must be undressed. Have a goblet of wine or water nearby. As a sign of beginning anew, you should take on a new consecrated name during this self-directed dedication process.

Open the circle, and have a small dish of anointing oil on the altar. In three sets, ring the bell nine times, briefly pausing after each group. Take up the anointing oil, and dip your index finger into it. On your forehead, draw a cross inside a circle in the position of the third eye, between your eyebrows. Over your heart, draw a pentagram. Replace the oil on the altar, and pick it up with your wand. (If you do not have a rod, you may use your index finger.) You should touch the oil to your genitals, right breast, left breast, and genitals, establishing a triangle.

Then salute and recite the following:
I am a simple seeker of knowledge and a lover of life.
I am both sacred and ethereal.
I now dedicate myself to you and your service.
I do this voluntarily and without pressure,
As you are the ones I have chosen to serve.
"And it harm none, do what thou wilt," says the Wiccan Rede.
My allegiance is to the gods.
Your protection is mine, as I pledge to protect you.
Let no one speak ill of you. We are one. So mote it be.

Tap the bell three times as you pour your offering into the libation dish. Then recite the following:

Blessed be,
For this sacred wine hath touched thy lips,
Let the dregs of this wine bind me
And hold me steadfast lest I should ever do anything to harm the gods.

Raise your drink to the gods. Replace the goblet, raise both hands high in salute, hold the wand over the altar, lower your arms, and ring the bell three times. Then recite the following:

By this, I take upon myself a new name
By which I shall always be known within this sacred space,
My place between the worlds.
Henceforth I shall be known as (new witch name).
So mote it, and to all, blessed be!

Draw a pentagram in the air with the wand, then kiss it and lower it. You may now sit and meditate; as you do so, you may receive some indication from the gods that you are indeed in touch with them—you will be awash with an inner feeling of comfort. Now, close your circle.

Four Elements, Four Quarters

Wiccans believe in the elements as the building blocks of life, as the forces of nature and creation. The universe comprises four elements: Earth, Air, Fire, and Water.

Throughout Wiccan and magical thought, these elements are infused throughout spells and rituals; secrets of the universe are encased in their vibrations. Each part has its energetic signature. Each also has several associations or correspondences. These correspondences are helpful in magic. The number of things associated with each component may seem surprising. Still, if you think back to the idea that the elements are the building blocks of life, it's not such a stretch. Therefore, if your goal and one of the elemental energies share traits in common, incorporating its characteristics into your spell work or ritual would strengthen your effort. According to Wiccan beliefs, spirits or otherworldly beings inhabit each element.

However, how Wiccans view these entities, their appearance, and their powers or properties will vary from tradition to tradition. According to ancient magical grimoires, which are the providence of ceremonial magicians and times older than Wiccan beliefs, spirits of the Earth are called gnomes, the air sprites are known as sylphs, the fire beings are called salamanders, and the water beings are dubbed undines. The gnomes are considered steadfast, reliable guardians of the Earth and sentries of its glories, like precious ores and gemstones. The sylphs inspire new thoughts and fresh ideas; these light and elusive spirits ride through the air and the sky. The salamanders live in the embers of the fire, and they ignite devotion, creativity, and vigor. The undines are lithe and full of grace and mystery, their passions constantly ebbing and flowing with their nautical home. Wiccans often attribute gods and goddesses to certain elements.

Elemental Connection and Attunement

Many Wiccans devote a lot of time and effort to exploring and aligning themselves with the elements to enhance their rituals and magic and to strengthen their habits and practices. Getting in sync with their spirits should be easy. They're everywhere and in everything, and we take them for granted. Paying attention to everyday phenomena, such as the elements, opens up many possibilities.

You can begin attuning yourself to nature's essence with the following exercise:

1. Go forth and explore.
2. Pick a start and end date, then start anew.

Starting today until the next solstice or equinox, make a conscious effort to notice and feel how the associated element works in your life and how it aligns with its season. For example, explore Winter and Fire, Spring and Air, Summer and Water, and Fall and Earth. Do so separately and together, beginning on the summer solstice, and keep at it until the autumnal equinox. Repeat, following the cycles through the year. Make notes in your Book of Shadows.

The Quarters

All life elements are present, an integral part of rituals and magic. The four cardinal points represent seasons and directions—the Earth is North, the Air is East, Fire is South, and

Water is West. Imagine a magic circle. Place the four quarters in their proper places around it, and it becomes a snapshot of life. Seasons spin around the sun, the circle of life, and drive Wiccans to work with natural patterns. They summon the quarters into their ritual rotations. If you start in the east quarter and move clockwise around the circle, you travel from dawn to midday to dusk to midnight, the cycle of a day; from new moon to waxing moon to full moon to waning moon represents the rotation of the moon. They bring the cycle of the seasons and all the building blocks of life into their microcosm —ascribing to this philosophy your will as a state of interstitial space and manifesting physical and spiritual planes.

Summoning the Quarters

Please note that the elements and the quarters are not the same, though expressly linked by symbolism. You can choose whether the quarters represent the elements or the elements represent the quarters. Wiccans often call the quarters in ritual just after the circle is drawn. Frequently, they will outline the circle and then go around it twice more, once sprinkling salt water and carrying burning incense, then once more bringing the four elements into the space. If the elements are already there before the quarters are called, attracting them is more accessible.

The pentagram is a five-pointed star with four points representing the elements, and the fifth symbolizes the unifying spirit. According to another theory, the pentagram represents a human hand, with the points representing the fingers. It truly is a powerful and positive symbol of creation and vitality.

An invoking pentagram is used to summon or invite the quarters' energies to the circle. When you call the quarters using the following method, you will draw an invoking pentagram in the air in each quarter. Visualize yourself pulling power from the Earth and inscribing the pentagram with the energy and your fingers or athame. To draw an invoking pentagram for Earth, begin at the top and draw down, then to the left, up, and right, and repeat as you draw the remaining points.

Align Yourself with Divine Energy

One of Wicca's greatest joys and responsibilities is connecting with the divine. Doing this does not require visiting a church or a sacred site. Anywhere you wish will do—everywhere is holy. Below is a simple ritual to familiarize yourself with the Great Mother and the Horned God. You may combine them into one or create one for each. You don't have to follow these instructions by rote. Use them as a baseline to get started. Have candleholders, a lighter, a candle (preferably gold, white, red, or silver), a trinket (perhaps a dreamcatcher or a favorite keepsake from childhood), a few dandelions that have gone to seed, several twigs, some blades of grass, and an athame.

1. Clean and clear your ritual space.
2. Ground.

Cast a circle. Do not call the quarters; the focus should be on the gods.

Sit in the middle of the circle with the candles in front of you. Light the gold or red candle, dig a little hole with the twigs, and place the dandelions and grass inside, or swish them in the dirt you dug up. Now, say something like the following:

> *I light this for you, O Lady of the Moon,*
> *Our Mother, Great Generous Goddess.*
> *I seek you, as I seek to gain your wisdom*

And pray that you are willing to open my dark eyes
To find understanding and knowledge.

Understand that you are just opening up dialogue with her—this isn't a call for the Goddess to enter the circle.

Tell the Goddess something about yourself—how you came to her, what you are searching for—or perhaps tell her your origin story and why Wicca compels you.

Close your eyes, inhale deeply, and focus on being relaxed. Once you've finished speaking, slowly and deeply inhale, exhale, and open your eyes. If nothing happens or you didn't discern the Goddess, don't worry!

Reflect on your connection, let your mind wander, and you will receive messages from the Goddess. You have made your intentions known to her by lighting the candle and stating your intent. Later on, it would help if you introduced your visions to her.

You may need to repeat this ritual more than once as you learn to hone and establish your connection. Patience is essential; Wiccan gods bestow all gifts in due time, so you can't coax or plead for things to happen precisely when you want them to.

Also, note that it may be easier to contact the God than the Goddess, and vice versa. One of them may resonate more strongly with you. Maybe you have a better connection with one deity for gender one day, or they symbolize another. When the reflections cease, or when you feel like you're finished, ensure you thank the Great God and Blessed Mother for their gift of wisdom.

Stand; take down your circle, and ground. Keep the flames burning for a bit, or snuff the candles. Try to take everything with you. If there's anything you can save for your altar later, like the grass or dandelions (or anything else that caught your eye), bring them home with you and place them on your altar. You can repeat the ritual later with the same candles and add other elements.

The Witches' Pyramid

The Witches' Pyramid is a magical principle or philosophy closely tied to the quarters. The pyramid contains four statements that express what you need to do to work practical magic and be a true Wiccan or witch. Each message is associated with a quarter, representing each quarter as a tier or level of the pyramid. Many witches study and work through each of the four statements to master their craft. They must also know that their magic or ritual will work. This is where you ask yourself if Wicca is right for you.

The East—to Learn

Air is linked to knowledge. Wiccans must know their will, intent, resources, and heart to work magic. You must understand that the spell or ritual will work and ask yourself if Wicca is right for you.

South—to Dare or to be Timid; That Is the Question

Fire is noble and linked to courage. To work magic, you must be audacious. You must gamble, take risks, be bold, challenge the status quo, and push your limits. Why did you choose this path? Why did you answer the call?

West—to Will Your Way

You are finding your way. Are you willing to listen to intuition and the subconscious? A Wiccan must know their will to perform magic. You gather your power and ensure your goal aligns with your choice or life purpose. Will you serve your higher purpose?

North—to Keep Silent

Silence is true wisdom's best reply. Earth represents stillness and cessation. To keep silent means that you don't discuss with others your magical work or the inner spiritual work you do. Who doesn't like to brag and post their success for everyone to be jealous of? That's why this level is often the most challenging.

Discover Wiccan Gods

In Wicca, the divine, or deity, is more significant than creation, and yet it is creation. There is an inherent divine quality to all things in Wicca. It is immanent in everything; it's inherently an alien notion, yet we try to grasp it in its totality. However, our journey with the gods opens us to new facets and possibilities. Darkness and light must be intertwined to be fully conscious and prevailing. The God and the Goddess represent, among alternative things, power incarnate, and the spark of life. Is it hard not to wonder if these gods are true-to-life, autonomous, self-governing entities? The immortal and also the God? They're the feminine and masculine halves of the divine. In Wiccan thought, the union of the eternal and these gods create the universe.

A lot of Wiccans would tell you that the gods are all of these things—which are by no means mutually exclusive—and more. Are they archetypes—symbols for universal themes that manage to pop up in the same way across cultures? Have they considered the forms that have taken on energy over time when people have revered them? Are they simply reflections of our psyches? Despite the apparent contradiction between Goddess and God and the awareness of a male and female duality (or oneness), the Wiccan Gods are not abstract to those who work with them. Wiccans have the responsibility and honor to establish a connection with the gods for themselves. The relationship between Wicca and the gods can be intimate and divine. But that means Wiccans must strive to work in unison with their gods, gain knowledge, and access them in a manner usually not attainable in mainstream religion.

You may know them already, so without further ado: Who are the Wiccan gods?

The Goddess

The Goddess of Wicca is the mother of all things, and the moon is her symbol. She is the Earth that gave birth to us, supported us, died, and accepted us again. She is a source of fertility, abundance, and compassion as a mother. Still, she also symbolizes the death that precedes rebirth. The Goddess has many faces, such as a waxing moon, a full moon, or a moon slowly melding into the sun at sunrise. She embodies these qualities: as energetic as spring, as ripe and fruitful as summer, as old and wise as autumn, and as dark and still as winter. Some Wiccans believe that the Goddess has three sides: a youthful girl, a fertile mother, and a wise sorceress, showing each of these faces as the year's cycles progress.

The God

The God is often depicted with horns to symbolize his relationship with animals, forests, and natural resources. He is a great hunter, lord of animals and forests, and protector of nature. He is assertive and wild, shrewd yet temperate. In other words, he represents the sun, without which the Earth (and the Goddess) would be barren. Many Wiccans link the God with the agricultural cycle: He is the spark of life that enables emergence from the Earth, ripe grains, and bountiful harvests. Some symbols of the God involve male phallic motifs such as arrows, daggers, lances, and rods. Other God symbols are the color gold, horns or antlers, and the stag, serpents, mature grain, and the sickle.

7

CREATING AN ALTAR OF YOUR OWN

Fundamentally, an altar is the same as a vision board. In essence, it is an entity that will center you, nurture your aura, and help you manifest your desires because it is tangible, interchangeable, flexible, and a way to stay connected with the maker, who transforms the physical into the metaphysical by creating a physical space for worship. Working with powerful and personal magic can be frightening. We connect with our bodies, our hearts, and our minds. This sacred space exists in both realms and holds objects, thoughts, and visions, reminding us that whatever we do anywhere bears fruit wherever we go. Integrity is paramount. We are all accountable for the wild wonder that is reached through the altar.

Our altars are our allies; they are not only a place and a thing but also a person with a spirit of their own. A working altar is explicitly designed for magical workings. It should be the least cluttered if you're using an altar specifically for magic. The evening is ideal for most workings; however, more intricate workings toward long-term goals might require an undisturbed setup for some time. You can access the higher spiritual levels you desire by engaging more senses and balancing your sense perceptions.

Why is an altar important? An altar can be defined as any collection of meaningful items you own. It serves three purposes:

1. It expresses the longing of your heart and the capacity of your soul.
2. It facilitates your devotion.
3. It provides a platform for spiritual practice.

Any spiritual altar is a symbol to remind you of who you are, where you came from, and where you are going! Your altar nourishes your soul. When creating an altar that is to be dedicated to your spiritual life, you put only things on the altar that inspire your spirit and bring to mind your ideals. Once you create your first conscious altar and discover how beautiful and sustaining it can be, you can make altars everywhere. You can't possibly go wrong bringing the blessings of the divine to whatever space you occupy. Because every altar establishes a home for what you enshrine on it, the divine will live there.

The Ready-Made Altar

Prepacked toolkits with herbs and tools are available online, designed explicitly for altars or shrines. Buying a prepacked kit will allow you to skip making a decision. Even though it may seem counterproductive to buy a premade kit, if it helps you mitigate anxiety, do it. You'll have all the herbs you need and won't have to hunt around. It's an excellent way to get your creativity flowing while creating custom incense blends for meditation. Clear your space of distracting energies, and create an environment where your imagination can run wild! These kits can contain charcoal tablets, a ritual bell, a miniature caul-dron, three or four candles, an assortment of salts, herbs like hibiscus or peppermint, and resins like ambrosia.

Safeguarding Your Altar

Too many little hands, paws, or feet around your home? What can you do to protect your altar? You can keep your altar in a curio cabinet, a repurposed IKEA drawer, or a bookcase. You can safeguard your altar with doors (and add a lock if neces-sary) to prevent children or pets from damaging it. If you insist on placing your altar out in the open, knowing that you can't always be there to supervise, then be careful about what you place on it. Setting the altar on a higher shelf, out of easy reach, and only taking it down when needed may be limiting for you. In addition to creating a powerful sense of importance and connection with your children, giving them their sacred space is also a good idea. Even a small desk with drawers to store their favorite toys can be enough. You can share yours with your children; they will learn to value and respect your space. And who knows? They may stop using your space as a play place!

Wiccans set up altars as decorative and devotional spaces around their homes or gardens. As places to house their devo-tion to the gods and a place to revere their particular items, altars allow Wiccans to express their faith, channel spiritual workings, and store their ritual paraphernalia. Wiccan altars can be as simple as a shelf with bark, acorns, leaves, and votive candles or as elaborate as a table with doilies, trays, crystals, incense, and flowers. Holy altars are permanently set up in the home or garden. In contrast, ritual altars are used only in a specific ritual circle.

The Surface

No rules exist about how big, small, fancy, or simple a Wiccan altar must be, so you can create one out of whatever suits you and speaks to you. I have seen altars made on end tables, coffee tables, shelves, file cabinets, planks, road cones, sewing tables, dressers and desktops, painted rocks, milk crates, garden gnomes, fireplace mantels, and old suitcases. If you are creating a divine altar, using a small table, your TV stand on your bookcase, or any flat surface you need, assuming it's easy to clean and meditate in front of.

Consider scrounging around thrift stores for an old end table if you have a few extra dollars. These are reasonably inexpensive. If you find one ugly, you can paint it or cover it with a cheap cloth. If you create a ritual altar, you will want something that can be taken down, stowed, or put aside when it's not used. I've found that trunks and chests are great because you can store your ritual tools inside and use the surface for the altar during a ritual. Using a simple table or surface in your ritual is also perfectly okay. I know plenty of Wiccans who move their coffee tables into their circle space for a ceremony and then put them back in the living room when they're done. Stability is also vital for a ritual altar, especially if you are moving around it or have burning candles on it.

Decor and Accessorizing

I love the fluttery feeling I get when I think about how to adorn my altar. If you want to, use a bought piece of fabric or fabric from an old quilt, or tear up an old dress, maybe the one you found at that garage sale. Once you've found a surface, decide whether to cover it or paint it black. Or match it with your favorite karma chameleon, some red, gold, greens, emblems, stars, fairies, or waves. You could even use your grandmother's lace doilies. Having so many choices is exciting. Also, adding foods or beverages associated with a particular Sabbat or deity is nice. I give offerings to my creators every day. They give me so much insight into my life's journey that it would be rude not to show them my appreciation.

When you offer something to a deity, you show them loyalty, gratitude, and love. Gods and goddesses will have their unique likes and dislikes. They are just like you and me in that respect, so keep their preferences in mind when planning your offerings. Sometimes I feel guilty about not being practical, getting caught up in buying the cutest and latest items for myself and offering food as an earthy, natural way to give thanks and offer penance. Remember to change these out periodically if they're not in some packaging so they don't attract bugs or grow mold. If you're building a devotional altar to a specific deity, you'll want to find items that correspond to them.

The God is the active principle. I will keep statues, candles, or male figures on the right side because the right hand is the prevalent hand. Any feminine dolls or figurines go on the left with goddess candles because the Goddess is the receiver. Next to the statue and candle of the Goddess, I put the chalice. Lastly, I prefer to place the water and salt anywhere that adds a natural balance and suits my mood. The broom doesn't go on the altar.

For example, I once made an altar for Meadhbh, the Queen of Connacht. She was a fierce and respected leader who led armies into battle on numerous occasions. I was captivated by the rumor that this Celtic Goddess was killed by a slingshot bearing a piece of cheese! I used a gray bandana with a black skull and crossbones, a purple light-shaped candle, a Buddha statue, a turkey feather, and a discontinued $5 bill in an SOS bottle. An old amber bottle.

Ritual altars often have decorative items on them. Still, it's more important to contain the tools and materials necessary for the ritual. Often, these items are put on the altar in symbolic places —for example, the censer is placed at the south edge of the altar because of its association with fire. However, sometimes it's much more essential to have the items laid out. Hence, they're easy to grab and use than having them in particular places. There is no right or wrong way to set up a ritual altar, but the widespread consensus is to face it north. I put the athame on the left as a homage to a singer I had a massive crush on as a child. After lots of practice, I'm adept at using my left hand, primarily since the athame is used often in the circle. I want it handy but take care not to injure myself. The utility knife is on the right to balance the athame. The center is in the middle, so it's less likely to be tipped over.

8

THE ALTAR AND THE CIRCLE

The placement of your altar can either benefit or hinder your practice depending on the surface, lighting, accessibility, and flow of the space. Your altar should be placed in the center of the circle (not necessarily aligned to any particular direction) to maximize viewing of the working and be the focus of energy. This makes moving around it by a large group relatively easy. We also respond well to gathering around the cauldron fire, whether natural or symbolic. Why is staging important? Here are some things I've seen that have caused awkward issues during ritual:

- The altar is placed on an outer wall of a room, but the circle (the working space) is more central, so the altar feels abandoned.
- The altar is placed not entirely in the center but not on the edge of the space, so people aren't sure whether they should go behind it or in front of it. Also, in this configuration, a large enough group of people will end up standing either in front of the altar with their backs

to it or on either side—unable to join hands if that's part of the ritual.

- The altar is set up in the middle of the room but not laid out to be accessible from both sides. (Just something to keep an eye on).
- The altar is placed in the center of the room where there are plans to dance or do exchanges that require weaving throughout the room—and the altar placement does not allow for enough movement/flow around it without causing issues.

So it's wise to consider the size of your space, the number of people you'll be working with, the amount of time you'll have to explain how the ritual will work, and how vital it is for your workings. If you want central focal points for your circle for everyone to gather around but don't have the space for something permanent—or access to a table—then consider something small and portable. It's not a secret that cauldrons can always double as altars, and there are reasons why stangs, or forked staffs, are so prevalent in witchcraft. They are visible and easy to decorate but take up very little space. If you're not tied down to a display of candles and proper tools, you don't need much stuff for your altar, do you?

Choosing the Right Spot

What if you've got a few options and are unsure which is best? Here are some exercises you can do to help tap into the energy of your space and get some divine guidance.

Dowsing

In addition to detecting groundwater with a divining rod, dowsing can also work in finding minerals, treasures, grave sites, and other hidden things. Dowsers connect with the spirits through Y-shaped branches (each hand on one end of the Y, the other end facing out or downward) that direct them toward a location. It's pretty easy to do. People may also use their wands. Try focusing on the question: "Where should I place my altar in my home?" Take a deep breath, and clear your mind. If you feel a pull on your rod, follow it carefully to see where it takes you.

Pendulum

A pendulum is another option if you cannot decide where to place your altar. To determine whether a site elicits a yes or a no answer from your pendulum, visit each location you are considering. Ask if it thinks this is the best place to put your altar and note the results.

Tarot

If you're familiar with the tarot, you could also pull a card to see if a location will work for you. Of the minor arcana, I'd be inclined to see most of the aces and tens as a yes, as they mark a cycle's beginning and completion, respectively. If you have multiple location choices, you can pull a single card for each to see if that gives you a clear answer. Another option is to ask the following: "Is this the best place for me to put my altar?" and pull four cards: three stacked—to express where you are coming from, what's happening now, and what can happen in the future, respectively—and the fourth card signifying the overall result of choosing that location.

On Meditation and Dreams

If you have difficulty remembering your dreams, you can meditate before sleeping. Of course, it might be better, in this case, to do a waking meditation. If your body allows it, sit cross-legged on the ground in the space or room where you intend to put your altar. Close your eyes, and visualize a taproot growing from your tailbone and reaching into the earth. As you imagine in your mind's eye your vines or branches reaching out to the place where your altar should be, think about a plant growing, expanding, and blossoming in your body's center. Once you have identified the space, return to your body and your ordinary consciousness.

9

PLACING THE ALTAR

In Wicca's mysticism, there are few absolutes. This is especially true when it comes to the orientation of the altar. Practicality often dictates where our altar (or altars) sits. Sometimes we face our altars according to instinct or divine guidance. Ritual altars have traditionally faced a certain way, but no set rule exists. There are many ways to arrange working altars in a ritual space. Still, they must face a specific direction during ritual action. In any situation, what matters most is what works for the individual witch; this is also valid for altars.

As the sun rises, the altar is traditionally placed in the East. But there are several reasons for orienting an altar in a particular direction. When you begin your circle castings and quarter calling in the East, you might find it helpful to ground yourself during the casting spell. If it feels natural, you might start there if it helps you get oriented.

Every ritual can symbolize a new beginning in the East, the direction of new beginnings. An altar's placement is also influenced by the moon rising east. Spirits of the East are often believed to be forces of wisdom, clarity, and inspiration that can be asked to summon the elements. So how about the South? Surely one can draw some energy from the south. For instance, it can express respect toward a solar deity in honor of the gods. Southern forces are also associated with ardor and tenderness. A south-facing altar at Beltane might help pull in some of those energies; this operation requires a large amount of passionate energy.

Performing rituals is a symbolic way of transforming our mundane existence into something more magical. Those who feel strongly connected to water may set up altars in the West to tap into its power. A west-facing altar may be especially appropriate during Samhain or whenever we want to connect with those who have gone before us. Traditionally, the North is seen as a stabilizing force. Having an altar facing North means the ritual will take on a solid foundation. The North is a place of power and connection to the natural world.

How you orient your altar is ultimately a personal decision, and no rule prevents you from changing the direction of the altar from time to time. If it feels right to you to have your altar face south from Beltane to Mabon and then the West for the remaining Sabbats, or if you wish to change your altar's direction every full moon, that's fine. Experiment with what works best for you.

An Altar Beneath Your Feet

Marking a floor to designate a sacred space is rarer nowadays, but what a beautiful way to dedicate a room! From wooden or concrete floors painted on to elaborate tiling and carpets, I have seen some magnificent chambers where the floor delineates the quarters or the elements. Adorn the space with other intricacies, such as tapestries, curtains, and other items you need to honor your traditions or personal practice. If you like this idea but aren't able to alter your home's floors, consider using an area rug instead—either a plain rug that you can add things to or a heavy canvas that you can paint on and lay out easily without tripping on it.

What Is the Ideal Size?

We all dream of having a personal temple—or at least a whole room dedicated to witchy things. But economic factors frequently present a challenge. Space is at a premium in most cities because of rising housing costs. Therefore, creating a fantasy room dedicated exclusively to witchcraft is hard. Perhaps you have roommates, a shared space, or small children. Or maybe you have enough space but don't want to be too extravagant. An altar space should take all of these factors into account. Size is not relevant, of course. It's how you use it.

Having a big, fancy temple room, you never use doesn't make you more spiritual than others or enhance your magic. While it may look cool, it doesn't score you any more points than someone who keeps their altar on a tiny shelf or in a small box. As a final consideration, is the altar suitable for the space and number of people you will be working with? You may encounter technical difficulties during your ritual if your altar is too small or too large.

What Room Should You Pick?

Here's a question I often hear: "Which room is best for an altar?" If you're living in a studio apartment, you are generally limited in your choices; it's usually determined by the layout and size of your space. If you have room to spare, it comes down to the level of privacy you want, the function of the altar, and the way you conduct your rituals.

If you have a fireplace, altars on the hearth are common and serve multiple purposes. If brews and recipes brighten your day, why not put your altar in your kitchen or pantry? The altar could be located there if the only privacy is in your bedroom.

If everyone in the household reveres accepts and requires access to the altar, then the ideal location would be a common area, like a dining room, living room, or basement. A bathtub is probably the best place for you if you enjoy your alone time and privacy is hard to come by. Move your altar away from your bedroom if it affects your sleep patterns too much.

10

SETTING UP YOUR ALTAR

The following lays out some guidance and a few considerations and options for you to ponder when setting up your altar.

Finding Space

It's up to you to decide the place for your altar. Setting up an altar requires thinking about how you will use it. Will you be standing in front of it for hours? Then it should be at a comfortable height for you, with proper footing underneath, like a rubber work mat or a thick, cozy rug with a pad beneath it. Would it be better for you to sit or kneel? Then you will want the altar to be at a height that works for those positions. Are you going to work on a table where you can easily see and move things with your hands? Channeling your energy already requires considerable concentration, so it helps if you feel comfortable. If your altar is too low, you may injure yourself. Ideally, you should be closer to a window if you need natural light. Placement near an electrical outlet is important if you want to plug in a string of lights. And consider fire safety if you use fire in your cauldron, incense, or candles.

Clearing the Space

Each time you decide to remodel and refresh your altar (maybe your moods change with the moon cycle or perhaps every year), you can cleanse the space by filling a bowl with water, adding a few drops of your favorite essential oils and maybe even some rose petals—as you use the water to clean your altar, visualize yourself filling the space with all the energy you want it to elicit. Regardless of what you are doing, sit at your altar every day. Generally, the left side of an altar represents what you want to let go of, and the right side represents what you want to attract. Make sure to have a corner for each of the elements. You might want to divide it based on different aspects of your life.

The options are endless. Put some gratitude in your space every day—this is one of the most practical things you can do, and it gives you an extra touch of magic. Accelerate your practice, record what you are grateful for, and frame it, or prop up your journal—maybe on wooden clothespins dangling off a hanger against a wall, surrounded by colorful shells and jagged stones. Or, every day, use blank pieces of paper to write what you are grateful for and place these in a glass bowl. Over time, that bowl fills up with all the good things you have noted, and you can refer back to them at random if you need to in stressful or challenging times. When you've finished using your altar, place any offerings or living elements you no longer need on your altar in your garden. Perhaps you have a candle there that you light while you write. You envision all the positive energies rising to fill your surroundings and life with gratitude as you gaze at the flames. An altar serves as a reminder to give thanks for what you have. Setting an altar can enhance a ritual, spell casting, tarot, or rune reading you are preparing to perform. Also, it adds direction and meaning to your practice, whether you make magic every day or only occasionally. You can also use an altar to focus on formal magical intentions. Intention setting and working together are beneficial to everyone involved.

You can find countless ways to bring more altar magic into your life. Imagine your tiny altar with symbols of wealth, coins, a quote or picture about perseverance, or an owl figurine reading a book. You can build that altar before your computer screen and meditate on positive outcomes while job hunting. Touching the items on your altar invigorates them, as they remind you of the elements or attributes they symbolize for you. Like cleaning day, maintaining your altars can be a thorough overhaul or as simple as light dusting. Cleansing, cultivating, and replenishing your altars clarifies and reinforces the reasons for building them.

Ways to Decorate

Once you've figured out how you want your altar to look and where you want its items to go, get a sketch or a photo into your Book of Shadows so you can easily recreate it next time. My go-to altar is set up from left to right. Across the top, I have a fire candle, a God figurine, and a dinner bell. Toward the center, I have a pentagram. Under the pentagram, I place a chalice with water, and my athame is under the chalice. On the right, I have a Goddess figure, an air candle, and a bowl with salt underneath. I have two or three plants on the bottom corners (bamboo shoots, pothos, philodendron, dracaena, anthurium plants, trumpet vines, or spider plant leaves). The middle section of your altar is the spell-working area. Find things that you love and that make you feel good. Leaving a little free space on your altar is crucial; resist the temptation to fill your altar with trinkets and knickknacks. Realistically, you'll find more and more things to add to it as time goes on—this being said, everything needs some breathing room. Imagine how stifling it feels to be in a room with too many things. In the end, too much clutter can produce an unfavorable and off-putting energy field. Keep your altar relevant by adding only relevant items—an altar enhances your craft, boosts your morale, and makes you feel good.

Your walls may not seem like the most exciting place to put something, but shelf space can come in handy if you're on a budget and don't have much money. A thick, solid shelf is better than a cheap particleboard shelf, especially if you plan to place heavy items on it. Also, check if your walls are made of drywall, which is easier to add shelves to. If you're renting, check with your landlord. Another option is a wire shelving unit; this can be extremely handy. It doesn't need to be mounted to a wall to be secure and can be quickly removed. You can also set the height of the shelves pretty much anywhere you want. A word of caution, though: add a smaller board or a liner tray smaller than the shelf to catch wax dripping, herbs, or ash from incense. You can also buy or make beaded or regular curtains to cover your altar—you can attach the curtains to a rod or use thumbtacks to keep the curtain in place.

Tables are some of the most prominent spots for altars, and their multipurpose function can be both an aid and a hindrance. Designating a table as an exclusive altar space can sometimes be difficult if it's your main table. Still, it can serve as an excellent temporary altar for special occasions. If you need an altar for a short period, an alternative is using a folding table or tray to give you the space you need and then store it when not in use. Accent tables can also be used as altars. Box shrines are mainly places of reverence. They are ideal for prayers and meditation honoring a particular deity, spirit, household guardian, ancestor, or the like. The shrine can include decorative items, such as a vase, crystals, herbs, a basket, or candles. The shrine doesn't have to be elaborate because it is more of a focal point.

Ways to Demonstrate

As a microcosm, we show a connection to nature, understand the impacts of climate change, and evidence a frugal mindset. We dedicate ourselves to developing a sense of identity and discovering what we can do to foster a sense of belonging. The creation of an altar allows you to receive guidance from the spiritual realm, regardless of which path you follow. It permits you to express your vision of the divine in any way you wish. You integrate the sacred into your personal life as you create your altar. It is a place for centering and rebalancing, making you more receptive to your subconscious thoughts.

How to Organize

Get everything off your altar(s), take inventory, look through your cupboards, chests, closets, and drawers, and clean a large area such as a counter, table, or floor. During this process, you'll probably discover tools and supplies you didn't realize you had. The most fun is picking out the essential items. Divide everything into three piles.

Your first pile consists of your main staples—your consecrated ritual tools and anything else you regularly use, such as statues, crystals, and lighters—and includes your current altar setup. Meditate on each item, and ensure it deserves its spot in this elite group.

The next pile is your secondary pile; these are items you need to have and be actively using. These items include backup supplies, ancestors' pictures, special-occasion items, oils you use occasionally, and things you no longer use but are reluctant to part with for sentimental reasons.

The final pile contains spent spell ingredients, candle stubs, broken and expired items, and tools you received, but that didn't work. Freshen the item up, dispose of it, or donate it. Often people keep too much witchy stuff around because they feel tossing it would be irreverent or unlucky. Use this opportunity to clean up your spiritual surroundings, as clutter hinders your aura. Ring a bell, sweep the air with your besom, shake away the cobwebs, and actively remove or repair old items, chasing away stagnant energy. You can also use this time to shed some love on your chosen tools. Anoint, charge, or reconsecrate them. Offer up a blessing for your rededicated space.

Now that you know what you have and where to find it, it's time to reset your altar. Organizing yourself will ensure your processes go more smoothly.

I try to cultivate my mind continually. Whether by reading or making a point to be present, it is crucial emotionally, intellectually, and spiritually that we grow from seed. We are on a quest to grow and thrive and seek the sun. We chase what sustains us, and sometimes we have some bumps. It is all too easy for our minds to become overgrown with seedlings of self-doubt with neglect. Our doubts manifest in many ways, such as negative habits, toxic surroundings, self-hate, or doubt. Taking care of negativity is not easy! A once thriving and beautiful mind can become ravaged if doubts are allowed to fester. In witchcraft, there is no room for negativity in spiritual dialogue. Weeding the garden of our soul is time-consuming and laborious but worth the effort. A healthy mind remains rooted in what is true. It processes its feelings and thoughts without the lens of guilt often associated with love and light.

Rather than a purely physical interaction, soul planting should be deeply emotional. The earth, in return, serves us with its bounty, energy, and itself. Incorporating this into your daily spiritual practice takes it from the realm of chores to one of enlightenment. Suppose you approach this exploration as a spiritual journey. In that case, you will learn as you go and become a sacred space to retreat from the noise and pressure of technology and daily life. What comes to mind when you picture a garden? Do you love the idea of nurturing plants from seedlings to mature plants? Or do you find yourself fascinated by maintaining rows upon rows of plants? What colors or decorations do you envision? In what ways will you protect your garden from predators? During this brief exercise, map out your thoughts and desires slowly.

As your mind wanders, allow yourself to pause and (physically) mentally find your space, a Zen point, and see what it feels like to be in it. When you are in the shower, with the water beading down your face, or when you go for a walk, you can take time to reflect, close your eyes, and feel the sun's warmth radiating along your skin as you go. In contrast to gardening, the sun's energy can fuel you. If you use it to your advantage, it won't hurt you if you do too much. Identify specific times when that resonates with you the most. What time of day do you feel at your best? Most importantly, learn what feelings, moments, or elements your spirit connects to the most. In which aspect do you feel most confident and in control?

Cleaning Up

It is relatively common practice among Wiccans to cleanse the area where they will hold their ritual, both physically and psychically, before drawing the circle. Cleansing the space has several benefits. First, conducting religious or magical work in a clean room is more respectful. It's less distracting to draw a circle and focus on a rite in a psychically clean area devoid of whatever unwanted energy has accrued throughout the day. Cleansing the space beforehand also helps focus your mind on the upcoming ritual. For some people, cleaning a room triggers the brain into a routine before the circle is cast. Begin by cleaning the physical area. If your rite is going to be outside, clear anything that might be in the way, like branches, children's toys, or lawn tools; rake up stray leaves and twigs; and check for anything you might trip over. If you like to perform rituals barefoot, check for sticker plants. If your ritual will be inside, move furniture if necessary, and vacuum or sweep the floor. Vacuuming and sweeping clean the floor and help break up and disperse energy. Using a special ritual cleaner made from pure water and specially selected herbs is a fantastic idea. Mixing up the solution is a magical act in itself. Don't put essential oils in it; they can take the finish off hardwood floors. Next, cleanse the space psychically. If you would like to do this, various techniques are available. Find one that feels appropriate for you and your living space.

11

USING THE ALTAR

You can create a harmonious atmosphere for a family gathering with a sacred space that allows everyone to feel at ease, especially if the attendees are of mixed spirituality or if you are using a space that you are unfamiliar with. You can create it without anyone else's knowledge by purifying and harmonizing the area's energy, removing distracting, harmful, old energy, and leaving a positive, comfortable feeling. Sacred space does not need to be dismantled like a circle does when you've finished your magical work. You can leave it and return whenever you choose, knowing that your sanctuary awaits you. When you're in your sacred space, you can still interact with the world beyond it—it doesn't set up a barrier as a circle does. When using sacred space, you make the existing environment holy instead of creating new surroundings. You remain open to the good energies in the area instead of sealing yourself away from them. To signal that your work here is finished, say something like this: "This spell is over—peace and blessings." How long does sacred space last? It depends on where you created it. If your sacred space is in a room of your home, its sanctity will linger longer than if you set up a temporary public space. The more often you use this space, the more you reinforce its sanctity.

How to Cast a Circle of Magic

Wiccan rituals and magical workings are most often conducted in circles. The circle is a sacred space created with energy and visualization, like a church or temple. The circle symbolizes many things, but one of the most commonly held ideas is that it is a space between the material and spiritual worlds since Wiccans walk, work, and worship in both. A circle is a place where both worlds exist, and neither exists. It is a place outside of time and space. Traditional in Wicca and for other practitioners of the craft is to cast a magic circle at the start of any ritual. The circle is a receptacle where all the magical energy you raise will be concentrated and a shield that keeps out any unwanted negative or distracting energy. Some witches cast a circle whenever they perform any ritual or magical act—even for consecrating tools. Others may save circle casting for larger, more elaborate purposes. In contrast, others consider the circle optional and may not cast one. Casting is recommended for beginners, as it can help you feel the energy you're raising in a more focused way.

There are many ways to cast a circle. You can physically mark the circle with candles, stones, herbs, and sea salt beforehand or allow the loop to remain invisible. Standing inside the circle, point your wand, athame, or index finger to the ground at the circle's northernmost point. Walk clockwise around the circle, continuing to point, and visualize your power charging the base at the circle's edge. You can do this just once, but walking the circle three times can be more effective, visualizing the power growing stronger with each rotation. Note: Make sure you have everything you'll need before you take this step, as it's not wise to break the energy of the circle once it's been cast!

Why Do You Need a Circle?

In addition to restricting sacred space, the circle's boundary works a little like your personal shield. When you draw the circle, you can decide what is allowed to enter it and what isn't. It can keep out everything or be like a medium that allows only certain things to pass.

Some Wiccans draw circles around themselves before doing visualization or meditation because they believe the circle will filter out extraneous sounds and energies that might interfere with their work. Others believe the circle prevents negative entities or energies from entering the consecrated space, keeping the sacred space safe. This idea has at least one of its roots in ceremonial magic. When they invoke spirits, ceremonial magicians may stand inside the circle for protection from whatever they're calling up. They may also stand outside the circle and cause the spirit to appear inside it for their own security or to keep the spirit bound in one place. Wiccans often raise energy in rituals to do magic. The circle keeps that energy in place until it is released to achieve its intended purpose. After all, you wouldn't want to go through all the trouble of raising energy only to have it seep everywhere before you can use it.

The circle retains heat from the bodies of the people standing in it, from any candles burning inside it, energy, or all the above. If you were to reach outside the circle during a rite, you'd notice that the air outside the ring is cooler than inside. The edge of the circle itself has an energetic feel too. I don't recommend reaching out of the circle; crossing the circle's boundary before the circle is "taken down" is considered bad etiquette. It disregards the sacredness of the space, breaks concentration, and may punch a hole in the ring that lets in (or out) things that the ritual goers didn't intend.

Hints and Tips to Prepare You for Casting a Circle

It doesn't seem very easy, but casting the actual circle is a lot simpler than you might imagine. Before I get to the instructions, you should know about the athame and the wand. You can draw a circle without any tools, but many Wiccans prefer to use one of these aids. In this case, the purpose is to focus the energy you'll raise to a point, like a pencil, with which you draw the circle. However, learning how to cast a circle without tools is essential. If you can do it without tools, you can do it anywhere, and that's handy in an emergency or when you need to do a spell or trance work on the fly. Doing it without tools also reinforces that the devices are just focal points and that the real power comes from the energy you draw and your mind.

Here's how to cast a circle:

- Decide where to begin along the edge of your circle. You can start at any spot along the edge you choose.
- Ground and lay your foundation.
- Imagine you are drawing energy from the earth's core through your roots.
- Raise your left or right hand, then extend the index and middle fingers and visualize the energy flowing into those fingers.
- Always move clockwise in a circle because it mimics the sun's path around space. Visualize a color representing the energy flowing through you.
- Move slowly, concentrate, and remember to breathe. Don't hold your breath!

- When you have finished and returned to your starting point, stop walking and solidify the circle by visualizing the entire boundary in your mind. Create a three-dimensional bubble around you instead of a two-dimensional circle on the floor. Hold the image in your mind briefly to strengthen it and make it real. Remember, energy follows thought, so visualization is crucial.

You've just cast a simple circle. You can try casting the circle without moving or using your fingers when you've practiced this and have the hang of it.

Once you're inside the circle, do not cross the boundary. You do not want to break up the energy. If you need to leave the circle and come back in, use the two fingers you used to draw the circle to cut a pathway into the boundary. When you return, redraw the line. Try not to do this except in an emergency, however. It's hard to maintain the circle's energy if you leave it. It messes up your focus on your work in the rotation.

To take down the circle at the end of your ritual:

Begin at your starting point, and move around the edge counterclockwise as you visualize drawing up the loop through your two fingers and pushing it back into the earth through your taproot.

Do not allow the energy to stay in your body.

Return it to the earth—ground after taking down the circle.

12

EVERY DAY ALTAR

Spellwork and rituals can seem complicated and mysterious. Feeling awkward is expected when starting on the spell-casting side of your journey. You will soon work with your intuition, developing spells and rituals that work for you. As your practice continues, you will learn spells from apps, books, or online forums.

Be not put off if a spell doesn't have the desired effect; this happens frequently and may need more work, but because one spell works for one person does not mean it will work for another. Some spells may not work; others may work wonderfully on the first attempt. You will soon discover a sense of doing things your way, working with your intuition, and developing spells and rituals that work for you. As with many things in life, practice truly does make perfect. Your accuracy and flow of magic, potions, and patterns will improve with repetition and experience. We all have to start somewhere, so I wanted to share what I have learned from close friends and some of my own trials and errors to help you get started. Walking is highly beneficial, especially for rituals where you must reach a destination in the woods or by a lake before practicing your magic. I walk to my destination (or if I'm at home, I visualize having made a mental walk), then lie down or sit cross-legged.

Keep an eye on your body. My body relaxes, and my eyes close. My remaining senses are heightened as my ears attune to listening to every sound around me—birds singing, wind rustling through the branches—I notice how the air smells, sense the rushing water, or feel the ground below me. As you relax, you may still be able to see shapes and patterns. Slowly visualize your ritual's intent, spell, and focus as you relax. You may notice changes in your body. What senses are engaged? Focus until you feel you can do no more—this may take a few minutes or almost an hour.

Spells for the Everyday Altar

Witches may or may not be concerned about the possible outcomes of their spells. Wiccans are bound by the tripartite law, so they may view the causes and effects of their magic differently. However, this doesn't mean that witches don't respect magical power, nor does it suggest that they are unethical. The tripartite law translates as the following: "What you sow is what you reap, not just once but three times." This is an excellent reason to ensure your motives are pure and genuine. In essence, this means there's a positive and equal reaction for every action, and for good or ill, one step can and often does come back to you—if not right away, then sometime down the road. Wiccans believe you create your destiny with your thoughts, words, and deeds. Because they subscribe to this idea, Wiccans tend to be more conscious of and conscientious in their behavior and thinking than many others. Although reincarnation cannot be validated, many Wiccans and witches seriously consider the karmic implications of their actions or inactions.

I want to highlight the core values of intimacy, connectedness, and assembly. As manifestations of the God and the Goddess, you and everyone you come in contact with are a manifestation of the divine and, therefore, sacred. As a result of connectedness, all things are energetically interconnected and interrelated. Healing or harming any life form anywhere on the planet impacts all other forms, even if they don't manifest physically. As followers of Wicca, we shouldn't be concerned only about our happiness and success but rather embrace our place as members of a global society and strive to pursue a harmonious life with all the people, animals, plants, and other life forms around us.

Magic and witchcraft has been the subject of numerous myths and superstitions. Some beliefs developed from simple misunderstandings. Casting a spell involves many things, such as images, words, movements, and objects. Still, the most fundamental component is the witch's will. When you cast a spell, you connect to the creative force that does not exist in the universe. Your intention not only fuels a spell but also colors it. Whatever its complexity, it relies on its power to achieve results. There's nothing wrong with doing gray spells—most spells fall into this category. It is absolutely not immoral or self-serving to somehow use our magical abilities to enhance our lives.

Nevertheless, the wise witch will always examine their intentions before casting a spell. Gray and black spells can sometimes have the same effects depending on your intentions.

Performing black magic does not necessarily involve the ritual of casting a spell. Many people perform black magic without even realizing it. If you curse someone or wish something terrible to happen to someone else in the heat of the moment, then you're performing black magic. When it comes to working magic, many different types of witches exist. Although some practices might not be wrong, they might not suit everyone. Do you feel comfortable casting the spell? What does your conscience tell you? Generally speaking, one can and should subscribe to some morally responsible principles.

By following a few simple rules as outlined below, you can avoid the problems, surprises, lures, and unpleasant consequences that sometimes accompany spell casting:

- Avoid casting spells that harm or interfere with the free will of others.
- Make sure your spells don't violate anyone's rights.
- Don't violate any taboos or ethics.
- Stay away from languages or symbols you don't fully understand.
- If you're ill, angry, or otherwise upset, don't cast spells, as this can adversely affect the outcome.

Spell for Daily Protection

In a banishing and purification spell, the goal is to remove a feeling, situation, or person from your life.

Materials required:

- Lighter
- Sea Salt or Pink Salt
- Small Glass Jar with a Lid
- Black Ribbon
- Cumin
- Dish for Burning
- Small Piece of Paper and A Pen

- An Offering or Small Item that relates to the person, situation, or feeling that you wish to banish

Process:

- Place cumin into your jar until it's about half-full; place a spoonful of salt on top of the cumin.
- On your paper, write down the situation, name, or feeling you would like to be rid of, then fold it up, place it in your dish, and burn it.
- Now, place the ashes into the top of your jar, on top of the cumin and salt.
- Fasten the lid onto the jar as tightly as you can. Before bed, shake the bottle as often as possible every night. Picture the situation or person moving away from you as you do this. Do this until the next full moon.
- On the day of the full moon, tie the black ribbon around the top of the jar.
- Take your jar and your offering to a river, the beach, or somewhere appropriate for disposing of the situation.
- Place or throw the jar into the water, and turn your back on it. Throw your offering over your shoulder into the water as well. Then walk away, and don't turn back or return to the area until the next full moon.

Spell for Blessing

Knowing what you know about magic, you can see how important goal-setting is in achieving your desired outcome. You do that every time you cast a spell. Once you've created a mental image of your goal, you can use willpower to realize it. Remember that the more tangible your goals are, the more likely they will materialize as you wish. If you feel unworthy, this will be reflected in your income and work situation.

In contrast, if you consider yourself deserving of a raise or promotion, your self-image will reflect your standing in the outside world. Do a brainstorming session, and write down anything that comes to mind. Promises can be general or all-encompassing, but having a list of a minimum of four to a maximum of twelve goals is essential. Don't start a spell if your answers are overwhelmingly negative. Instead, turn those negative answers into positive terms and affirmations. What will your positive affirmations be? State your dreams in terms of pledges. Read your declarations thrice daily, morning, noon, and night before bed. By repeating your wishes, you imprint them on your subconscious. As soon as you've accomplished one objective, replace it with another. Here is a simple one to get you started:

By knot of one, the spell's begun.
I yearn for my magic to flow like the dew by the knot of two.
Now, by three, I pledge my life to thee.
Nevermore, by four, the joy of receiving your blessings I shall no longer implore.
On five, my spirits begin to revive.
My fingers numbing, only knot six, grace my feet to kick and stir up reflex.
Seven, feel rested and whole.
'Tis eight, thine honor and wisdom dost mold me.
Lastly, the knot of nine, oh, what joy divine.

A Spell for Some Satisfaction and a Little R-E-S-P-E-C-T

Are you tired of humming about being pushed around? Do you feel at odds? Does every interaction leave you angry and unsettled? It's down to you, so use this spell to restore your sense of dignity if you've been mistreated recently.

Gather the following:

- Cinnamon Essential Oil
- Pen, Pencil Crayons, or Colored Markers
- Two Orange Candles
- A Candleholder or a Dish (let some wax melt onto the dish first, then press the candle down and hold until firm)
- Dried Bay Leaves (whole or shredded)
- Lighter
- Paper And Tape (or bottle or jar)

When you are ready, begin as follows:

1. Cast a circle around the area.
2. Make a circle with a dot in the center of both candles (be gentle, as you do not want to break the candles).
3. Rub the essential oil into the candle (but avoid rubbing the wick or the candle won't light), and set it in its holder or apply it to the plate. Take three or four deep breaths, and allow the scent of cinnamon oil to infuse you with feelings of confidence, faith, and enthusiasm.
4. Light the candle and sprinkle (or place) the bay leaves around it. With pencil crayons or colored markers, write on the paper the words' respect,' 'freedom,' "peace of mind," or any other relevant terms that come to mind. Next, draw images to represent your sense of power, status, and honor. When you're finished, put a drop of cinnamon oil on each corner of the paper.
5. Extinguish the candle, and gather up the bay leaves.
6. Tape the bay leaves together (or place them inside a jar), then place them on your desk, beside your computer, on a picture frame, or inside a fake plant. Or you can keep

them hidden in a safe place and out of view. Don't forget to keep your drawing close by so you can look at it often. Take a few deep breaths, inhaling self-confidence.

Daily Altar Meditation

Meditation can best be described as listening with your mind's ear. It is the art of listening to one's inner self or to a higher, creative power. When appropriately used, meditation leads to personal advancement. Meditation is the simplest of all the techniques for spiritual progress, and it can be practiced by individuals or groups. By practicing meditation, you quiet the conscious mind, with which you worry about life and everyday activities. Meditation lets you channel your subconscious, which is responsible for involuntary bodily functions and reflexes. These things may be meditation, but you can also fail at meditation if you approach it with the wrong technique—and certainly, if you do not approach it at all! Concentrating on your third eye, an inch above your eyebrows is believed to help you focus your energy. The direction in which you focus your eyes also plays a vital role. Turning your eyes upward, above the horizon, enables you to relate to the energy in your higher consciousness and your spiritual power. Focusing your eyes straight outward links to your conscious mind, while focusing downward puts you in touch with the subconscious mind.

When performing meditation, select a comfortable position of your choice. If your spine is straight, you can assume any position—sitting on the floor, perching on a chair, or lying down on your back. Conventionally, one should be in the lotus position, but comfort is key. The more comfortable you are, the better you can concentrate on your energy and mind. The space you choose to perform your meditation must be quiet, and the best spot will be your cleansed and censed circle. However, if you select another area, cleanse the space and sense it as you did with your ring. While facing a specific direction in meditation is not necessarily essential, facing east is often suggested. Again, your comfort is the most important, so if you have a better view in another direction, feel free to orient yourself that way instead!

Additionally, you may choose the time of day you meditate based on your position, the direction you face, and the space you choose. However, it is best to stick to that specific time of day every day to keep your meditation consistent. Choose a convenient time that will be quiet, peaceful, and attainable each day. Meditation needs to be done consistently to remain successful.

Here is a step-by-step meditation method:

1. Lie comfortably on your back, not slouching or bending your spine.
2. Lean forward, allowing your head to rest on your chest. Breathe deeply in and out three times. Return to your upright position.
3. Roll your head backward, inhaling and exhaling deeply. Do this three times. Sit up straight again.
4. Let your head fall to the left as far as you can. Take three deep breaths before returning to your original position.
5. Rotate your head as far right as you can. Take a deep breath in and out three times. Straighten up.
6. Make three counterclockwise circles with your head.
7. Allow your head to fall forward a second time, but turn your head clockwise in a loop this time. Do this three times. Return to your original erect position.
8. Let your lungs fill with air by taking a few deep breaths. Focus on breathing through your nose. Inhale

for a few seconds, and then loudly exhale through your mouth. Repeat three times.

9. Inhale slowly and fully through your right nostril while holding the left closed, then repeat with your left. Let your stomach expand, and then hold your breath for a moment.

10. Inhale briefly, then gently and slowly exhale through your mouth, flattening your chest—this is a good exercise for clearing stale air from your lungs. Repeat three times.

11. Breathe slowly and thoroughly through the left nostril while holding the right closed. Repeat with the right nostril. Let your stomach expand.

12. Hold your breath and exhale slowly through your mouth, flattening your stomach. Do this three times.

13. Now that your body is relaxed and you are breathing normally, concentrate the thoughts in your mind and imagine your entire body surrounded by a globe of white light. Envision and feel the energy charge your whole body.

14. Now, it is time to focus your attention on your toes. Relax them, and feel the tiredness or the tension slip away. Do the same with the balls of your feet, the heels, the arches, the ankles.

15. Relax your entire body, focusing on releasing the tension from it a section at a time. Work up your whole leg, groin, buttocks, and spine through your stomach, chest, upper limbs, throat, face, jaw, and chin. Don't forget your eyes and even your scalp. The intention is to relax every nerve and fiber in your whole body. The relaxation technique ends at your forehead.

16. Now, focus your energy on your third eye. Allow your eyes to roll up if possible. Try to go deeper and deeper into the third eye as far as you can. With all the

concentration you can muster, release yourself from
the material world, and yield to a magnetic pull if you
feel it. There is no need for prayer or visualization; you
must concentrate on relaxing your entire body. Allow
your energy to flow from inside outward and to a
higher power.

Whatever sensations you experience, move into them and
through their source. Initially, your conscious mind will be
undisciplined, and it may be difficult for you to quiet it, like a
nagging child. However, with practice and consistency, you will
eventually start to see results in the form of a deepening intuition. It is common for beginners to have difficulty remaining
still for more than a few minutes at any given time.

Also, it is normal for your mind to want to wander and for you
to feel like fidgeting. You'll notice that you're easily distracted,
whether by a massive itch that suddenly needs scratching or
your grocery list. Ignore all these things as best you can, and
soon you will be in control of your mind and your body. It is a
complicated process—you are transitioning from allowing your
mind and body to rule over you to you ruling over your mind
and body.

When you are spent, ending the meditation correctly is important. In the best interest of your physical well-being, you end
each session of meditation by reawakening your conscious and
physical self—this is done by performing the relaxation technique in reverse, which means pulling away from the third eye
and proceeding down the length of the body, section by section,
commanding them each to become awakened and vibrant. You
will likely be somewhat surprised by how pleasant you feel
after meditation using the proper technique. Clearly, there are
not only spiritual benefits but physical benefits as well!

13

RITUAL ALTAR

Throughout human history, people have been using the natural cycles and rhythm of the earth to celebrate life and death, marriage and divorce, and health and illness. Each season comes with unique celebrations and processes within the year's rhythm. Time is as circular as it is linear. Calendars were based on the cyclical motions of the sun and the moon. The Wheel is followed to incorporate this circular, continuous, rhythmic flow into daily life. To be attuned to the moon's ever-shifting cycles, align your magic, and feel peace and comfort in the rays of rhythm and change.

Sabbats, days of power, are a way to honor the ebb and flow between the shifting roles of the God and the Goddess, whether as mother and child or as two coconspirators and partners and back again. While under the same umbrella as Sabbats, the Esbats focus solely on the Goddess in her role as the moon and her three faces: Maiden, Mother, and Crone.

Gerald Gardner played a vital role in revitalizing Wheel-of-the-Year festivals. During the mid-20th century, Gardner devised a

Wheel of the Year marking solstices and equinoxes as well as four Celtic fire festivals: Samhain (Winter Nights, Halloween, and Pagan New Year), Imbolc (Saint Brigid's Day and Candlemas), Beltane (May Eve and May Day), and Lughnasadh (Frey Fest and Lammas). During creation, only the four Celtic holidays were named.

Due to this initiative, we have a mixture of Celtic and Germanic-influenced holidays. Solstices and equinoxes were initially named based on the seasons and functions of the day, not by distinctive names. Aidan Kelly revamped them in the 1970s; today, they are known as Yule, Ostara, Litha, and Mabon.

The Sabbats

The following describes the meanings, customs, and traditions of the Sabbats.

Samhain

Samhain is the first festival in the Wheel of the Year. Also known as Halloween, All Hallow's Eve, and the Witches' New Year, Samhain is the middle point between the autumn equinox and the winter solstice. Celebrations tend to last several days (and, in some cases, a few weeks). Many modern pagans and Wiccans refer to it as Samhain. However, it is a Celtic reconstruction from more ancient Celtic-Irish practices. Samhain is marked by a thinner veil, reverence for the dead, and harvesting plants and livestock. The word 'Samhain' means November in modern Irish and Scottish Gaelic, but it has been suggested that the phrase also takes its root from the term "summer's end."

Samhain is the big spindle or spoke on the Wheel that transitions us from birth and growth cycles to the cycle of death.

While celebrated by many on the night of October 31, Samhain is observed on November 1—this is not a hard-and-fast rule, with many pagans celebrating in the more conglomerate harvest holiday Halloween style, which ranges from October 31 through November 5. Being a midpoint holiday, however, the actual date of Samhain does change. It can be calculated by finding the day between the autumn equinox and Yule. One of the most common phrases about Halloween and the Samhain season is that "the veil is thinning." This term has become popular in spiritual and pop culture circles—but what does it mean? Many people believe that a veil separates our world from that of spirits. However, a few times a year, like during major holidays, this veil becomes thin—noticeably so when deceased loved ones are remembered. Think about conventional New Year's Day. How many people make wishes and resolutions?

What is any harvest holiday without a Thanksgiving as well? The heart of Samhain is not associated with any particular deity. Still, it encompasses all gods, goddesses, and other deities joining us during this thinned veil and closer connection. However, some specific gods and goddesses like to make their presence known during this time of year. This is not to say that these particular deities must be worshiped or acknowledged, but if you do happen to work with any of them, now is a great time of year to set up a task-oriented altar. The veil is thin this time of year. Our ancestors and recently lost family members are more accessible to contact and include in our daily lives. One of the more common Samhain traditions is what is known as a "dumb supper or a dinner with the dead. A dumb supper is a meal that memorializes and remembers loved ones and ancestors and invites them back into our lives for a meal. Dumb suppers can be held at any time of the year and for any reason, but they are usually observed on Samhain. There are two main ways to perform a dumb supper. A dumb supper, or silent supper, is traditionally held in complete silence (hence its name) to show reflection and respect.

Typically, a meal is prepared, and different place settings are allocated at the table for deceased loved ones and ancestors. The meal is conducted in all seriousness, and each person considers their private memories with those who are no longer with us. Having a wandering spirit join you at your table is unlikely at this time since only those of your blood are invited.

A dumb supper can also be held in an Irish style. This three-course homemade meal is loud, full of great food and alcohol, and a celebration of life. You want your relatives to feel as loved and joyous as they were here. Three is the number of the Maiden, Mother, and Crone, so serving three courses symbolizes the season's spirit. Samhain's dumb supper is always based on a lamb meal, just as Thanksgiving and Christmas are always centered around turkey or ham. As much as possible, I use in-season local food or produce from my garden rather than out-of-season or processed foods.

The first course can be warm and comforting, like creamy butternut squash soup and soda bread; the second course is perhaps a lamb Wellington with okra and cranberries. The final course can be a berry cream or yogurt parfait. Use whatever your favorite fall comfort meals and desserts are. Samhain was a time for our ancestors to cull their livestock for the harsh winter months ahead, and there was often a surplus of meat and dairy products at this time of year. I encourage you to be as authentic to that as possible. There are different ways to set the table for a dumb supper, whether hosting it alone, with your immediate family, or with a larger group.

Whenever I am alone for a dumb supper, I sit at the foot and make place settings in all other seats for specific people. It is essential to serve these plates and places before you come to yourself, being the last of the living line at the table. The head/foot of the table on your left side should be made in tribute to your family, while your right side will be for your partner. Our family will always be on our left side, symbolically closest to our hearts and minds, while still connected to the family. In group settings, you follow the same principle as outlined above and have the place setting for your family directly to your left—this will mean that every second place setting is made available. Your family's settings should be adorned with items and articles they particularly liked, such as alcohol, food, candy, and photographs if you feel so inclined— this is to bring the spirits of your direct family members to join the congregation of celebration and commemoration. Your line is unique; make sure they feel that way through your words and actions during this time.

Yule

Yuletide is a celebration with tendrils that encircle various cultures. Thoughts of Yuletide invoke both light and darkness. The dark side of the modern Wheel of the Year is centered on Yule, a Germanic festival (also known as the winter solstice). Once upon a time, Yule wasn't linked with the winter solstice but rather the season. From holiday garlands, wreaths, confections and treats, bright and wondrous lights, and keeping warm via the fire of Yule logs, the pagan roots of this season are still an active part of secular and spiritual life.

When we talk about the Yule season, we think it starts during the first week of December. Nearly every spiritual practice, though, can appreciate the importance of the year's darkest day, the descent we took to get there, and the rebirth coming into the new year. Yule is English in origin, deriving from the Old English word 'girl,' which translates to Christmastide. The term is also said to stem from the ancient Norse word 'Jól,' a pagan winter solstice festival. Modern Yule, mainly from an English and Anglican-influenced traditional holiday, grew from its roots in the heathen Germanic and Norse practices. The pagan Yule occurs on the literal day of the winter solstice. At the same time, the heathen Yule begins around December 20 and lasts until about December 31. Seems familiar... almost Twelve Days of Christmas familiar, right?

Timing is one of many apparent differences. Festival days can also vary. Today's Yule always takes place on the winter solstice but can be observed the night before through to the morning after. Yule is the darkest time of the year when the veil is the thinnest between the living and the dead—outsiders may mistake this for Samhain. Still, its essence and intent are entirely different. Yule is a celebration of reflection and a time for relaxation. Today, it emphasizes the renewal of the sun. Yule is the sun's rebirth, which follows the year's darkest night. It is not a sad time, nor does it commemorate the dead or acknowledge them; it is full of hope, promise, joy, and rebirth. We are blessed to have a wealth of festive myths because no culture, religion, or practice possesses the essence of Yule. While some might say that certain practices are specific in origin, our nomadic European ancestors shared many of their beliefs, giving us a general, almost uniform approach to the winter solstice season.

Imbolc

Imbolc is associated with the sun, fire, life, water, and divination. It is the midpoint between the winter solstice and the spring equinox. However, the festival is celebrated over multiple days and is less time-sensitive than Samhain. A celebration of Celtic origin, Imbolc is originally thought to have been honored on February 1. However, it is now observed on February 2, which merges it with the Candlemas celebration of the Catholic Church. Currently, the festival of Imbolc begins on what is known as February Eve, January 31. It continues through the end of February 2. The Christian Church converted the festival into what is now known as the Feast of Saint Brigid.

The Goddess Brigid was noteworthy to the Celtic people during the last phase of the winter season. Brigid is not only the Goddess of childbirth and healers but also the Goddess of the hearth and fire. During Imbolc, it is believed that her light will help take the darkness out of winter and rejuvenate the earth with the warmth and light of the sun. Imbolc brings the first thoughts of the earth's fertility and the possibility of spring on the horizon. Secularly speaking, the beginning of February brings love, lust, maybe even welcoming newborns (furry or human), and time spent inside to escape the cold. Much of how popular secular culture celebrates love during this time of year is reflected in the activities of the gods.

In the growing light of spring and as the sun rises, Imbolc serves as the perfect time to renew, center, and celebrate your growing devotion to your craft and the gods. The connection between fertility, purification, and spiritual rebirth is derived from the word 'February.' Dedications involve simple public or private ceremonies where people intend to study Wicca and honor the gods. Having an initiation ceremony is when you become a true Wiccan and stop being a devotee. The ceremony might serve as a reminder that we are entering the season of fertility. The wind isn't blowing as hard, and you're beginning to spot some budding trees. Perhaps it would be better to consider it a time of potential fertility when the earth ceases to be lifeless and begins to awaken. Fire symbolizes warmth, the spark of life, and the coming of the light. Several Sabbats involve fire, but Wiccans speak of their internal fire at Imbolc. You may want to hold more candle ceremonies to encourage the light and warmth to grow—this is also a time of purification in the sense of sloughing off the darkness of winter and getting rid of extraneous stuff that keeps you from your spiritual potential.

Ostara

Ostara, believed to be Roman in origin, predates Wicca and Christianity. It is thought that Caesar established it to mark the start of the tropical year. In some ways, the Wiccan spring equinox is like Easter. On the secular side of Easter, people celebrate with colored eggs and chocolate rabbits. Eggs and rabbits are two of the few things you can have on the table in mixed company, symbolic of fertility and new life. Easter is also when rabbits bring eggs to the table. Christians celebrate Easter as the day Jesus conquered death and rose from the tomb. Light triumphs over darkness as the sun rises over the horizon in the Northern Hemisphere on the spring equinox. During the Wiccan spring equinox circle, flowers are often used to represent all that is blooming around us and being beautiful, available, and symbolic of what is entering the power of the Wiccan God as spring approaches. Wiccans must understand the polarity of light and dark during the spring and fall equinoxes to maintain a sense of balance.

A balance exists between work and play, ego and humility, compassion and strength, and heaven and earth. Some Wicca traditions hold that the Goddess and the God are married at Ostara. As you look outside, you'll see that the world is fertile, pregnant with the potential for life just about to emerge from the ground, just at the beginning of a new season of life in nature. It is not just our physical spaces that have become dusty but also our minds. It is the time of the year when we tend to ourselves, profoundly affect our spiritual well-being, and restore the balance in our physical and spiritual spaces by decluttering, cleaning, and tidying up. Do we possess mastery over our possessions, or do our possessions possess us? We breathe, but perhaps our possessions hinder us and don't allow us to decide what to devote our energy to daily. We have the choice to maintain lots of things or fewer things. The physical clutter directly reflects our internal chaos when we have lots of stuff. Cluttered physical space often translates into a chaotic spiritual or mental life, as reflected in countless reality shows. This concept is found in almost every self-help book, and it's true. Decluttering is not simply about decluttering; decluttering is about letting spiritual growth and energy flow through your space.

If you think things have gotten out of hand, don't worry. Do any basic decluttering you like. For example, light a candle, and place it on your working altar when you have a few free hours. You might ask your higher powers for their help while you do this. Keep the candle burning as long as possible, preferably letting it burn straight through. Take a few minutes to meditate. Take stock of what stresses you the most in your physical environment, grab those trash bags, and tackle them. After putting everything in the bags, use a broom to sweep the dirt clockwise, moving it out of the room and out the front door. Afterward, prepare your mop by adding a bit of salt and a handful of cleansing herbs in Florida water to a bucket of cold water. Mop in a counterclockwise motion. Let your floors air dry completely.

Beltane

As one of the four Gaelic fire festivals, Beltane is associated with bonfires more than any other. The Beltane fire is traditionally lit on May Eve or Beltane (May 1). It contains bundles of nine types of wood, chosen for their symbolism and associated attributes: apple, birch, fir, hawthorn, hazel, grapevine, oak, rowan, and willow. In the past, these sacred fires have been used for ritual. In their more modern form, Beltane fires and festivals are a reason to celebrate the joy of living and being alive. Say a chant with me:

Toward the east. Hallelujah!
Oh, hail, wise sylphs of the east! This beautiful fire burns for thee.
My bell enchants thee. My bell respectfully and dutifully calls.
Hear it ring, soft and genuine.
Purge and complete this holy rite. Please accept our thanks.
Now it is time to go. Thank you, and farewell!

Some people find comfort in a burning ceremony during late spring to early summer, which is cathartic and relieving. This ceremony is conducted between May and July. It involves people bringing letters, articles, books, pictures, videos, and other items connected to traumatic or painful memories. They each stand up and discuss what they are burning, why they are burning it, and what they hope to achieve. What should you do? You'll need a large fire (preferably in a bonfire or pit), a pen, paper, and a seat. First, take a moment to center yourself in your body and turn inward. Think about any aspect of yourself that doesn't serve you anymore. Changing something easy to achieve is an excellent way to begin. Beltane symbolizes the beginning of spring and the return of longer days.

You may feel overconfident because Beltane falls right in the middle of the Taurus season. Despite the bravado you feel now, if you work in any capacity throughout the day, you will encounter situations and people you cannot control. Creating a special place for spirituality can help you unwind from life's physical and mental responsibilities.

An old saying is that a witch's spiritual life revolves around adjusting the sails, not the wind. Not everyone can handle this power loss or struggle, and they feel crushed under the weight of that particular brand of pressure. The good news is that what you decide to do with your stress will change your situation. Being able to turn off the world when you choose to is a big accomplishment, and with practice, we all can achieve it. Why not go to a spiritual retreat? You can work on techniques to build bridges into your mind to retreat to when life gets too overwhelming. This technique can apply to various situations.

According to some Wiccans, Beltane is one of the two times of the year when the fairy court moves. Male and female dancers wrap the ribbons around the pole, holding the ends until the entire rod is bound and separated. It marks the sexual union between the God and Goddess and the harvest, which means food for the next year and the beginning of a new cycle for Wiccans. Beltane's primary purpose was to promote procreation; it isn't a holiday to be taken lightly despite its trappings of fun and games. On this holiday, it was common for young women to prance about all night with their lovers, and many would become pregnant. Bonding among tilled fields makes them sanctified as well. Witches who work with the fae might leave out libations, such as cake and milk, to honor and appease them. Beltane's most famous symbol is the Maypole, where a garland of flowers is hung.

The God and the Goddess are mature, strong, and in love. There is a wild, feral, unpredictable side to the God, but he also has a gentle side. He is the Green Man, entirely dressed and covered in foliage. He is lord of the forest and of growing things. You might be attracted to the Green Man at Beltane if you wander through the woods under the moon. Equinox is a playful time, and Beltane is joyous. Often much feasting occurs at Beltane celebrations. Some Wiccans include beer because it is made of grain, associated with the Green Man. Like the spring equinox, Wiccan Beltane rites are full of flowers and greenery, and women and sometimes men wear garlands on their heads. Like Imbolc, Beltane is a fire festival, and outdoor Wiccan ceremonies often include a bonfire. Couples join hands and jump over the fire together to increase their fertility. Be sure to build a small bonfire, avoid wearing anything that will catch fire, and have a fire extinguisher nearby. The rites for a seasonal Beltane altar may include flowers, greenery, ribbons, phallic symbols, and symbolic sex rituals. It is not uncommon for established couples to sneak off and go a-Maying after the circle is over in anticipation of creating the magic of conception, a robust tradition of Beltane.

Litha

Our gods appear in full glory after death, sleep, and rebirth in fall, winter, and spring. Traditionally, Litha was the last name of June and July, or it is said to be derived from the word 'lithe,' which means mild. Litha was used before the mid-20th century to describe the Midsummer festival, not as it is today. The summer solstice occurs at Litha, or Midsummer, the second spoke on the light side of the modern Wheel. It is the longest day of the year in the Northern Hemisphere when the sun is farthest north.

In addition, many of the themes associated with Beltane will apply to Litha and the rest of the summer Sabbats during this time of year and other festivals that share the same motif. It is associated with fire festivals in the light half of the Wheel, just like Beltane, and large bonfires are lit to symbolize the sun, sensuality, life, and fertility.

Death is prevalent in the dark half of the year, while life plays a significant role in the light half. The beauty of nature, the flowers, the blades of grass, and the way the sunlight peeks through the trees and reflects on the streams are enough to take your breath away. What could be more vibrant than loyalty, laughter, and fecundity? Isn't it weird how your friends are all constantly in a fighting mood? No, maybe like a trying week; you've had it with their aggravation and their urge to discipline. That's okay. Saturday night's all right, all right, all right, all right, ooh... maybe you'll decide to all gather around 7 p.m. and perform this ritual. I suggest (if you didn't already catch my hints) this is best performed on a Saturday, as it is the end of the week, so you can release all your stressors and get a good night's sleep and relax (or perhaps go on a quick hike early Sunday morning). Alternatively, you can do this on Sunday or any other day that suits your schedule as long as this ritual can help you promote self-care.

You may adjust the following as needed, weather (locale) permitting. If you don't feel comfortable making a bonfire, use the light from your phone or a pocket flashlight. You should identify and prepare a list of your personality traits you feel no longer help or are burdensome to you or keep them in mind to create vulnerable freedom within the boundaries and energy of the Litha season. Separate your emotional attachment to physical items that weigh you down spiritually, physically, and emotionally. If it helps, donate these burdens instead of throwing them away. Don't torture yourself by holding on to things that hurt your shadow. Release that attachment to the pain and what it symbolizes. You are no longer there and can let go of it. All you need is love (is love... is love...) and the following:

- Paper

- Bonfire (or other light/fire source)
- Flowers
- A Pen or A Marker
- Whatever you may have that is heavy on your mind
- Water to put out the fire, if applicable

To start, light your fire.

Walk around the fire in a circle, ensuring it burns safely from all angles, or walk around the ring four times with your light source. Allow your mind to become one with the flames and your power to merge with the fire. This ritual works well if you are in your natural state; however, if that isn't safe, the fewer the clothes, the better. Make a list of everything you are giving back to the universe. Once you have written each trait down, repeat the following:

Love and grace to you, Higher Power.
Release me from the weight I place on my shoulders.
Love and grace to you, Higher Power.
I commit myself to reducing this burden as well. It cannot stay the same as it has.
Guide me now, Higher Power, with love and grace.
Thank you for guiding me through the garden of my mind.
Be my companion as I navigate the waters of my soul.
Walk beside me along the trails of my youth.
Just as you have gone before me, you will continue to do so after me.
I put my trust in you. So, blessed are you.

In the final stage of the ritual, you will put the paper in the fire. Keep doing this until all the pieces are in the fire. After doing this, place the flowers you brought in your hair. Imagine that your most precious parts are at the center when you complete this ritual.

Lughnasadh

The first of the three harvest festivals is Lammas or Lughnasadh. Lughnasadh is the festival that marks the midpoint between the summer solstice and the autumn equinox. Historically, this August 1 date has moved around a bit. Lughnasadh is now commonly observed during the first weekend following August 1. Lughnasadh occurs after Samhain, Imbolc, and Beltane. Lughnasadh is a feast celebrating the harvest in the Northern Hemisphere when the first grains and fruits are harvested. Items on a Lughnasadh altar could include a sickle, bread, wheat flour, a sheaf, or even beer for Wiccans.

This holiday emphasizes sacrifice—not a human or animal sacrifice but the knowledge that everything has a price and that one thing must be sacrificed to allow another to be born. The word 'Lughnasadh' is considered an amalgamation of Loaf Mass, a celebration of the first wheat harvest in Europe. Grain, or wheat, is viewed as a symbol of the God. Some Wiccans mark Lughnasadh as the death of the God when God gives up his life force to sustain humanity and begins to descend to the underworld, where he will later be reborn. An enduring element of this holiday is the sacred European king, Lugh, associated with it. According to this myth, the king represents the people and God, while the land represents the earth. While the sacred king myth may not be factual, it is deeply rooted in Lughnasadh's mythology and symbolism. Lugh was the Celtic God of light and the sun, and he carried a magic spear. Lughnasadh is generally a happy Sabbat but tinged with the knowledge of death and the coming darkness. Both associated with Lugh, competition, and games are common at this Sabbat. As the king was the people's emissary in times of famine, it was customary to sacrifice him to bring about a harvest. Typically bread was sometimes baked and then sliced into the shape of a man to represent the king's sacrifice.

As a Wiccan, you may prefer the symbolism of John Barleycorn. According to English folklore, he represents the crop of
barley harvested each autumn and the great drinks made from
barley, such as beer and whiskey. Several old folk songs
personify the barley as John Barleycorn and honor his demise
and rebirth as beer. In reality, beer is more fun at a Lughnasadh
Sabbat than a loaf of bread. What we enjoy at the harvest
comes at a cost; death means life to all of us. All Sabbats mark a
turning point in time. Lughnasadh occurs opposite Imbolc on
the Wheel of the Year. At Imbolc, Wiccans celebrate the potential of the light and the God. At Lughnasadh, they celebrate the
culmination of that potential.

While I wish I had a beer gratitude and blessing ritual to share,
here's a bread ritual instead. As anyone who practices gratitude
regularly will tell you, showing appreciation for one's blessings
is essential—attracting what you wish to receive. You can use
this simple ritual to thank the gods for their blessings during
this season of fruits. Seven candles are ideal, but feel free to use
more if you can.

Gather the following:

- Seven Candles (you should include at least one gold,
  one yellow, and one orange candle in your group; the
  size of the candles doesn't matter)
- Flowers (if you can't buy fresh flowers, artificial flowers
  are fine, too, as long as you intend to reuse them; you
  can choose from sunflowers, coneflowers, bush daisies,
  tickseed, chrysanthemum, or yellow daisies)
- Loaf of Freshly Baked Bread
- Pen and Paper

Arrange the candles, pluck the petals from the flowers, and let
them fall as they may (if you forget to bring a pen and paper

before you pluck, envision a blessing). Put your bread on a consecrated plate or napkin, and light at least three candles. Take a moment to write down seven to eleven of your greatest blessings over the past month or two. You can also note down small blessings to balance out the list. Once you have made your list, light the remaining candles, and don't forget to thank the gods before you light your paper. Then rip off a chunk of bread, raise it to the sky, and say the following:

Oh, gods and goddesses, thank you for filling my dark heart and eyes with a fraction of your blessings. I allow thy nourishment to sustain and guide me. I am grateful and blessed to be able to partake in a morsel of your body.
Blessed be.

Mabon

Mabon is considered one of the lesser observances on the Wheel of the Year; it is the last festival in the light half of the Wheel and is thought to be named after the Celtic Welsh god Mabon. Mabon is a god of light and was the son of the earth's mother goddess Modron. In Lughnasadh, we watched as the God acknowledged his final decline before the cycle of death and rebirth. Mabon is when death is upon us; we do not fret, though, as we know he will be reborn as mote be the cycle, as it has been and always will be.

As the second harvest festival, this is the time for joy and cele-brating the fruits of one's labor. The English harvest festival Harvest Home is celebrated on the last day of September with decorations and corn dollies representing the spirits of the fields. Harvest End and Harvest Home commemorate the end of the harvest; these separate celebrations are held on the exact dates of Mabon. Ancient folklore says that when one plants an apple in memory of Asmodeus, the devil who tempted Eve, the name should be engraved on the earth and canceled with a cross. Quaint, right? It reminds me of several school trips where my classmates and I spent time on a farm. As a child, I loved to watch people climb up a ladder or even join other children in shaking the trees, as getting apples ourselves was so much more fun. I cherish those memories; usually, I would be the first in line when we "planted" apples (buried for compost or for the pigs to eat) or carried the ones we picked to bring home afterward. Apples traditionally symbolize abundance, prosperity, love, and magic and are considered an enchanted part of the harvest. It is a great time to visit a fair, buy candied apples, or bake an apple pie. Rather than banishing Lilith, we call upon her and ask her for fertility, protection, and guidance. We embrace her intelligence and safety.

Apples can help bring prosperity, their seeds can be used for protection, and they can be used as an offering during harvest. If an apple is cut in half horizontally, the seeds often form a pentacle shape; while admiring this, I was inspired by random internet searches and a few memes, which led me to find the following wonderful idea. Drumroll, please! Apple incense/candleholders! I am not the inventor of this idea. You're probably wishing you thought of this yourself—I know I do! You can also use apple-scented candles; it's a lovely way to add fruit to your altar.

You will need the following:

- Red or Green Apples (a little tart and a little sweet, a totem to Lilith rising and theoretically bestowing rare goodness)
- Coned Incense (or a tea-light candle)
- Permanent Marker or Sharpie
- Paring Knife, Corkscrew, or Apple Corer
- Lemon Juice

Hold the candle to where on the apple you want it to go and mark the spot with the marker. Insert the apple corer into the apple at this spot, use a paring knife to make the hole bigger, or add pieces of the apple back into the area if it's too big. You can use the corkscrew if you only have incense sticks. With your paring knife, carve out where the candle will fit. Once the skin and top portion of the apple have been removed, put some lemon juice on its flesh to keep it from browning. If using a tealight candle, drop it in and enjoy your new candleholder. These incense/candleholders can last up to a few days.

The Esbats

Here is a brief overview of how the energies may affect you over the cycle to help you tune in to your magical intent.

New Moon

The new moon marks the beginning of the lunar cycle. As darkness draws to a close, you can slowly begin to feel and align yourself with the moon's rhythms. As the thinnest of silvers forms, begin to dream a dream. It's okay to be unsure of what the dream will be. Begin imagining your journey toward completing a specific goal, whether adopting a new pet, moving into a new apartment, or finally taking the leap and applying for your dream side hustle. Use the new moon to start various opportunities to hone your intuition and gain self-confidence. Work spells to enrich and enhance your goals. Traditionally this is the best time to use the magic to initiate and start new projects.

Full Moon

The full moon is the most potent phase of the lunar cycle; even people who don't believe in magic are compelled to recognize the full moon's energy, such as erratic moods, heightened emotions, and altered sleep patterns. Understanding the magic allows you to take advantage of these lunar energies and direct them to serve your purpose and make your desires a reality. You are in tune with the Mother realm of the Triple Goddess, and her nurturing ways are manifesting your desires. The magic tends to be more potent before the moon becomes full; as it lends itself to helping you focus your intentions and circumstances. However, don't do the work if you cannot perform your ceremony in the morning or before midday. Cast your spells more enthusiastically once the sun has set and the moon has risen. You'll still notice an improvement in your clarifying psychic abilities.

Waxing Moon

When the moon has transitioned from waxing half to waxing full, you will notice that your intentions from the previous waxing and new moon phases are beginning to be fulfilled—a magical period when more effort leads to greater fulfillment. If you are receptive enough, the universe is keen to offer you other desires and wishes. Any new workers may benefit from an extra energy boost to urge them toward their goals. Document how different bursts of energy aided or detracted from your intuitive inclinations. Call on the goddesses Nuit, Asteria, and Luna during this time.

Waning Moon

The waxing half is when projective, active energies ramp up. The waning half is accompanied by amplifying the receptive, passive energies of release and decreasing illumination. You should focus on more practical goals, such as getting rid of unhealthy habits, eliminating self-doubt and despair, and ultimately remembering to appreciate the blessings of happiness, as this time is for banishing and releasing negative influences. Depending on your views, your list may be long or short. No matter what, tackle only the concerns that are tumultuous and overbearing. There is no such thing as eliminating all of life's problems; instead, remove as much negativity as possible. As the moon is in full effect at night, when waning magic is most effective, you reinforce positive habits and simultaneously accept that things are beyond your control. You want to align with the crescent that rises around 3 a.m.

CONCLUSION

It's fair to say the actual work has just begun! How do we use the opportunities to change the world positively? What would happen to your practice if tomorrow you were forced to move? Can you support your craft in a new setting with different lands, spirits, elements, and climates? Or would you find yourself struggling like a fish out of water, trying to connect using methods that are no longer effective for where you are? I hope I have helped you develop a holistic approach to creating altars that you will love using. You take the time daily to push yourself and grow deeper in your craft. We are the only ones responsible for how far we go on the pathway that we walk.

In these uncertain times, I'm glad to have you hear my voice and for you to allow me to play a small part in your journey. I hope you take this light, protect it, and are willing to share your light with others who practice this wondrous craft. Each person has a unique and divine connection to the universe, making their narrative special. As we evolve, there will always be something new to bring to the table in the world of spirituality. My perspective melds bits of science with bits of history and narratives that are uniquely my own. Throughout my study of different altar arrangements, I have always tried to learn as much as possible and be open to sharing my talents with others and using them to help myself and others. I try even when my mind bids me not to or when I am dissatisfied or constrained by my altar.

The central aspect of Wicca is the religious ritual. Understandably, you are drawn by the magic; remember that magic plays only a part—and for some, it is a big part. Yet magic is a capricious force that doesn't always work! When your magic doesn't work, you need to look inside yourself before looking at external reasons for failure. What was wrong with your mechanics? Did you use the right herbs and crystals? How long did you steep your tea? Was that rum or Florida water that you just added to your bath? Before you invoke another spell to fix the one that didn't work, try to ascertain what went wrong before; everything needs to be considered. Believe in yourself, and remember, there are no absolutes when it comes to magic. It behooves you to acknowledge that the gods know better than we do. I suggest repeating a magical ritual five times over 2 to 4 months before giving up. What you try to bring about by magic may not fit the plan. Sit at your altar and do nothing when your spell doesn't work. Just breathe. Then and only then should you examine it to see if there might be some other entirely different approach you could try, and if that doesn't work, accept defeat.

As this book concludes, I wish you and your family blessings to partake in another spin around the sun as it rises, heavy with potential, and then recedes and almost vanishes. Then, again and again, when we think we have lost everything, we will discover ourselves in our place among nature. A witch's destiny is not to assume the role of master of nature but to serve as a protector and an advocate. Preserve your craft. Spread love.

Wishing you the best on your journey, knowing that God and Goddess will always be there for you. I wish you well on your path, knowing you will always have a place to turn to for help.

It is so with life.
No strife.
No matter where I go.
Do I feel the presence of the gods?
Yes, I do.
They surround me.
They are part of me.
We are one.
We are one.
Everlasting.
Such is life.
No strife.
No matter where I go.
Do I feel the presence of the gods?
Yes, I do.
They surround me.
They are part of me.
They surround me.
They are part of me.
We are one.
Everlasting.
Let no evil come to pass
In that place of purity.
Within and all around me.
Toward good, I strive every day.
Love unto all things.
So mote shall it be.
Forever.
There shall be no evil.
Pure is the abode of all goodness.

In me and around me.
For the sake of goodness, I work.
In me and around me.
Loving all things.
So mote it be, always.
Softly falls the rain upon the fields below.
These sounds grant me the solitude I seek with enchanting, peaceful
sounds that lull the heart and flow smoothly and calmly, gentle
whispers in the wind.
The gentle rain falls, not bending a leaf,
The rain will wash away all grief.
A calm ensues.
Peace and love follow.
A freshness descends from the clouds.
As all evils flow out, all that remains is fresh and clean.
Let no negativity enter.
With gratitude, once more, this room is pure.
Oh, love, I am blessed to see and find all around me.
So sure and so soft, granting me wisdom to further engage in my
rituals.
As peace fills the depths of my heart and my soul.

Don't stop here! The path toward knowledge and enlightenment continues. Don't miss out on the priceless insights waiting for you in the Practical Magick series.

mojosiedlak.com/practical-magick-series

BIBLIOGRAPHY

Alden, T. (2020). Year of the witch: Connecting with nature's seasons through intuitive magick. Weiser Books.

Alexander, S. (2008). The everything Wicca & witchcraft book: Rituals, spells and sacred objects for everyday magick. Adams Media.

Alexander, S. (2014). The modern guide to witchcraft: Your complete guide to witches, covens, & spells. Adams Media.

Bado-Fralick, N. (2002). Mapping the Wiccan ritual landscape: Circles of transformation. https://core.ac.uk/download/pdf/213811084.pdf

BoomerTheWitch. (2020, August 17). Witchcraft offerings. Human Witch. https://medium.com/human-witch/witchcraft-offerings-821c69d1a78a

Buckland, R. (2018). Wicca for one: The path of solitary witchcraft. Citadel Press.

Chamberlain, L. (n.d.). The Wiccan altar—the tools of Wiccan ritual. Wicca Living. https://wiccaliving.com/wiccan-altar/

Chamberlain, L. (2014). Wicca elemental magic: A guide to the elements, witchcraft, and magic spells. Occult Shorts.

Chamberlain, L. (2015). Wicca herbal magic: A beginner's guide to practicing Wicca herbal magic, with simple herb spells. Wicca Shorts.

Chamberlain, L. (2021). Wheel of the Year to the cycles of the moon, magic for every occasion (the Mystic Library, Book 8). Sterling Ethos.

Conway, D. J. (2000). A little book of altar magic. Crossing Press.

Crystals. (n.d.). Wicca Wiki. Retrieved April 30, 2022, from https://wicca.fandom.com/wiki/Crystals

Dragonsong, E. (n.d.-a). How to smudge for purification. Www.wicca-Spirituality.com. Retrieved May 22, 2022, from https://www.wicca-spirituality.com/smudge.html

Dragonsong, E. (n.d.-b). Sacred scents—Wiccan incense. Www.wicca-Spirituality.com. Retrieved May 17, 2022, from https://www.wicca-spirituality.com/sacred-scents.html

Dragonsong, E. (n.d.-c). Wicca altar basics. Www.wicca-Spirituality.com. Retrieved May 18, 2022, from https://www.wicca-spirituality.com/wicca-altar.html

Estrada, J. (2021, April 30). How to make your very own Altar at home. Cosmopolitan. https://www.cosmopolitan.com/lifestyle/a36302874/how-to-make-an-altar/

Fredette, M. (2020, February 28). Parenting, baby names, celebrities, and royal news. Cafemom.com. https://cafemom.com/lifestyle/how-to-witchcraft-altar

Gruben, M. (2016, July 27). Messy altar? Four simple steps for organizing your witchy stuff. Grove and Grotto. https://www.groveandgrotto.com/blogs/articles/organizing-your-altar-supplies

Gruben, M. (2017, July 13). Circle-casting basics: All you need to know about magick circles. Grove and Grotto. https://www.groveandgrotto.com/blogs/articles/circle-casting-basics-all-you-need-to-know-about-magick-circles

Heldstab, C. R. (2012). Llewellyn's complete formulary of magical oils: Over 1200 recipes, potions & tinctures for everyday use. Llewellyn Publications.

Herstik, G. (2022, May 19). Ask a witch: All about candle magick. Nylon. https://www.nylon.com/life/ask-a-witch-candle-magick

History.com Editors. (2018, March 23). Wicca. History.com (A&E Television Networks). https://www.history.com/topics/religion/wicca

How to cast a circle. (2021, June 30). WikiHow. https://www.wikihow.com/Cast-a-Circle

How to set up a simple pagan or Wiccan altar. (2020, May 16). WikiHow. https://www.wikihow.com/Set-up-a-Simple-Pagan-or-Wiccan-Altar

Kunkel, S. (2019). Wicca book of spells and witchcraft for beginners: The guide of shadows for Wiccans, solitary witches, and other practitioners of magic rituals. Educational Books.

Lipp, D. (2003). The elements of ritual: Air, fire, water & earth in the Wiccan circle. Llewellyn Publications.

Magical tools in Wicca. (2020, July 10). Wikipedia. https://en.wikipedia.org/wiki/Magical_tools_in_Wicca

Mankey, J., & Zakroff, L. T. (2018). The witch's altar: The craft, lore & magick of sacred space. Llewellyn Publications.

Nice, H. (2019). Wicca: A modern guide to witchcraft & magick. Seal Press.

Phidipus, T. (2020, March 2). How to set up a Wiccan or pagan altar for beginners on a budget. Exemplore. https://exemplore.com/wicca-witchcraft/Wiccan-Altar-Set-Up-For-Beginner-Wiccans-or-Wiccans-on-a- Budget

Pollux, A. (n.d.-a). 19 dynamic witchy altar decorations and how to use them. Wicca Now. https://wiccanow.com/19-witchy-altar-decorations/

Pollux, A. (n.d.-b). Create a powerful witchy altar with these 7 top tips. Wicca Now. Retrieved May 19, 2022, from https://wiccanow.com/witchy-altar-set-up/

Rite of Ritual. (n.d.). Creating an altar. Rite of Ritual. Retrieved May 17, 2022, from https://riteofritual.com/blogs/blog-posts/creating-an-altar

Sabin, T. (2006). Wicca for beginners: Fundamentals of philosophy & practice. Llewellyn Publications.

Smith, D. (2016, March 26). Looking for witches and Wiccans in history. Dummies. https://www.dummies.com/article/body-mind-spirit/religion-spirituality/wicca/looking-for-witches-and-wiccans-in-history-201047/?keyword=looking%20for%20witches

Smith, D. (2022, February 16). Wicca and witchcraft for dummies cheat sheet. Dummies. https://www.dummies.com/article/body-mind-spirit/religion-spirituality/wicca/wicca-and-witchcraft-for-dummies-cheat-sheet-209055/

Starrs, S. (2016, January 18). Creating sacred space: How to set up your own altar. Sarah Starrs. http://www.sarahstarrs.com/the-blog/2016/1/18/creating-sacred-space-how-to-make-your-own-altar

Stickelman, A. (n.d.). 91 altar room ideas (altar, witch aesthetic, sacred space altar). Pinterest. Retrieved May 7, 2022, from https://www.pinterest.ca/archaney3/altar-room-ideas/

SunKat. (2016, May 27). Incense herbs. Witches Moon. https://witchesmoon.wordpress.com/2016/05/26/incense-herbs/

Syrdal, K. (2018, August 13). Here's everything you need to know about setting up your witch altar for spells, meditation, and more. Thought Catalog. https://thoughtcatalog.com/kendra-syrdal/2018/08/heres-everything-you-need-to-know-about-setting-up-your-altar-for-spells-meditation-and-more/

Tfrecipes.com. (2017). Wiccan protection prayers recipes. Www.tfrecipes.com. https://www.tfrecipes.com/wiccan-protection-prayers/

Tragic Beautiful. (n.d.-a). Find your spark: Creativity toolkit. Tragic Beautiful. Retrieved May 10, 2022, from https://www.tragicbeautiful.com/collections/witchcraft-all/products/find-your-spark-creativity-toolbox

Tragic Beautiful. (n.d.-b). Resin incense: What is it & how to use it. Tragic Beautiful. Retrieved May 20, 2022, from https://www.tragicbeautiful.com/blogs/style-blog/resin-incense-what-is-it-how-to-use-it

Tragic Beautiful. (2019, May 28). Altar essentials. Tragic Beautiful. https://www.tragicbeautiful.com/blogs/style-blog/altar-essentials

Van, N., & Vernon, K. (2017). Practical magic: A beginner's guide to crystals, horoscopes, psychics & spells. Running Press.

Wally. (2021, June 4). How to cast a Wicca ritual magic circle. The Not So Innocents Abroad. https://www.thenotsoinnocentsabroad.com/blog/how-to-cast-a-wicca-ritual-magic-circle

Walsh, M. (2013). Wicca candle spells: Simple magick spells and rituals that work fast (Wicca and witchcraft). Ingram Publishing.

We'Moon. (2011). Understanding altars: What is an altar, and how to bring altar magic into my life. We'Moon. https://wemoon.ws/blogs/magical-arts/understanding-altars-what-is-an-altar-and-how-to-bring-altar-magic-into-my-life

Wicca. (n.d.). Wicca Wiki. Retrieved April 29, 2022, from https://wicca.fandom.com/wiki/Wicca

Wiccan altar cloth. (n.d.). Etsy. Retrieved May 21, 2022, from https://www.etsy.com/ca/market/wiccan_altar_cloth

Wiccan altar dish. (n.d.). Etsy. Retrieved May 22, 2022, from https://www.etsy.com/market/wiccan_altar_dish

Wiccan altar dish (n.d.). Etsy. Retrieved May 7, 2022, from https://www.etsy.com/ca/market/wiccan_altar_dish?ref=pagination&page=3

Wigington, P. (2018, December 11). Setting up your magical altar. Learn Religions. https://www.learnreligions.com/setting-up-your-magical-altar-2561940

witchyshelly. (n.d.). Spells (protection spells, witchcraft spells for beginners, witch spell book). Pinterest. Retrieved May 19, 2022, from https://www.pinterest.ca/pin/462393086750815568/?mt=login

Wright, M. S. (2020, September 25). Beginning Wicca: Types of altars. Exemplore. https://exemplore.com/wicca-witchcraft/Beginning-Wicca-Types-of-Altars

Wright, M. S. (2022, March 31). How to make a Wicca altar on a dollar store budget. Exemplore.com. https://exemplore.com/.amp/wicca-witchcraft/Wicca-on-a-Budget-The-Dollar-Store-Altar

Zimmermann, D., & Gleason, K. A. (2006). The complete idiot's guide to Wicca and witchcraft, 3rd Edition. Alpha.

ABOUT THE AUTHOR

Monique Joiner Siedlak: Author, Witch, Warrior.

With storytelling infused with mysticism, modern paganism, and new age spirituality, Monique awakens your potential. Initiated into the craft at 20, her 80+ books explore the magick and mysteries of life.

A Long Island native, she now calls Southeast Poland home but remains a citizen of Mother Earth.

Beyond her pen, Monique craves new experiences and cherishes nature, advocating for animal welfare.

Join her captivating journey as she transports you to enchanting realms and empowers your own transformative path. Unleash the dormant magic within and embrace the extraordinary with Monique Joiner Siedlak's evocative words.

To find out more about Monique artistically, spiritually, and personally, feel free to visit her **official website.**

www.mojosiedlak.com

facebook.com/mojosiedlak

x.com/mojosiedlak

instagram.com/mojosiedlak

youtube.com/@MoniqueJoinerSiedlak_Author

tiktok.com/@mojosiedlak

bookbub.com/authors/monique-joiner-siedlak

pinterest.com/mojosiedlak

MORE BOOKS BY MONIQUE

African Spirituality Beliefs and Practices

Hoodoo

Seven African Powers: The Orishas

Cooking for the Orishas

Lucumi: The Ways of Santeria

Voodoo of Louisiana

Haitian Vodou

Orishas of Trinidad

Connecting with your Ancestors

Blood Magick

The Orishas

Vodun: West Africa's Spiritual Life

Marie Laveau: Life of a Voodoo Queen

Candomblé: Dancing for the God

Umbanda

Exploring the Rich and Diverse World

Divination Magic for Beginners

Divination with Runes

Divination with Diloggún

Divination with Osteomancy

Divination with the Tarot

Divination with Stones

The Spiritual Empowerment Series

Creative Visualization

Astral Projection for Beginners

Meditation for Beginners

Reiki for Beginners

Manifesting With the Law of Attraction

Time Bound

Healing Animals with Reiki

Being an Empath Today

Crystal Healing

Communicating with Your Spirit Guides

Life on Fire

Healing Your Inner Child

Change Your Life

Raising Your Vibe

Get a Handle on Life

Get a Handle on Stress

Get a Handle on Anxiety

Get a Handle on Depression

Get a Handle on Procrastination

The Holistic Yoga and Wellness Series

Yoga for Beginners

Yoga for Stress

Yoga for Back Pain

Yoga for Weight Loss

Yoga for Flexibility

Yoga for Advanced Beginners

Yoga for Fitness

Yoga for Runners

Yoga for Energy

Yoga for Your Sex Life

Yoga to Beat Depression and Anxiety

Yoga for Menstruation

Yoga to Detox Your Body

Yoga to Tone Your Body

The DIY Body Care Series

Creating Your Own Body Butter

Creating Your Own Body Scrub

Creating Your Own Body Spray

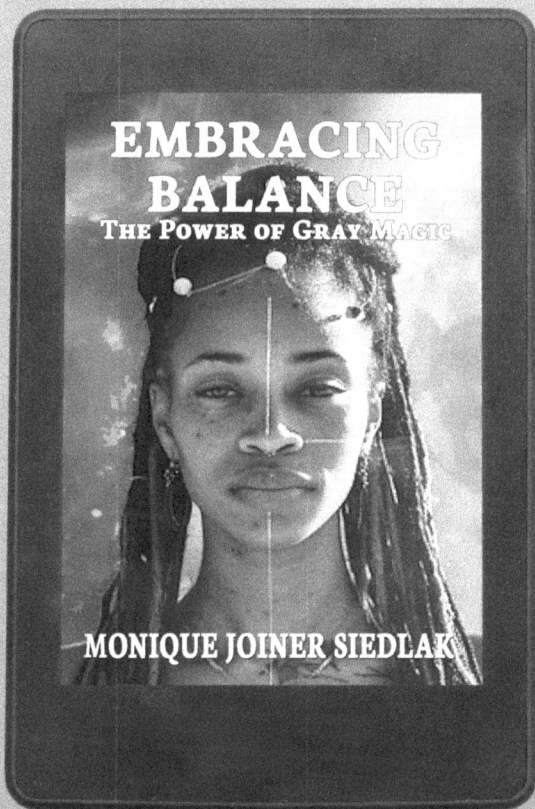

SUPPORT ME BY LEAVING A REVIEW!

goodreads

amazon

BookBub

nook

Rakuten
kobo